This Book is Dedicated
To the Memories of

My Son
TREVIS KENT MILLER
August 7, 1962 - July 14, 1983,
Who did not live to achieve his promise,

My Mother
MARION REINHARDT RYMER
July 20, 1903 - November 27, 1992,
and
My Father
CHARLES ALBERT RYMER, M.D.
November 28, 1900 – May 1, 1997,
Both of whom exceeded their promise!

Acknowledgements

The production of a book is like the ideal relationship between lawyer and client, a team effort. This book was produced with the assistance of the following team players to whom I express my deepest gratitude:

Lawyers: Gertrude D. "Trudy" Chern, Rebecca Heinstein, Nancy Ruth Hoffman, Athena Mishtowt, and James Preston;

My terrific daughter, Stefanie Miller, who plays many roles in my life;

My dear friend Kay Talbot, PhD., for her detailed editing;

My designer and illustrator: Norman Lubeck;

Many members of the Northern California Chapter of the American Academy of Matrimonial Lawyers, whose suggestions helped me to improve this second edition;

My long-time communications advisor: Florence Beier of Beier & Associates.

Table of Contents

Part I Procedure and You

Part II   Substantive Family Law

Introduction

This book is about divorce in California. It's also about how to save money. You can learn from this book about how to pick the right lawyer, how to work efficiently with a lawyer, and even how to provide better informed emotional support to friends who are going through the divorce process.

This is not a "do-it-yourself" manual. The advice of a competent lawyer, preferably a Certified Family Law Specialist, is well worth the cost, compared to the risks of trying to diagnose and treat your own case. This book explains how the divorce process functions, what you can do yourself to move through its maze smoothly, and how to cooperate with your lawyer so that you and your lawyer can work effectively as a team.

Most people are appalled when they discover how much a divorce costs. Yet often their instructions to their lawyer are to blame. A major difference between the client's expectations and his or her actual position in the eyes of the law can lead to serious mistakes. Then, if the client also ignores the lawyer's counsel, financial disaster may follow. Three examples illustrate this point:

Arnold said he wanted a complete break with his wife. He wanted to pay no alimony and certainly did not expect to pay any of her lawyer fees. His lawyer told him that a man of 45, in good health and earning $100,000 a year as he was, would surely be ordered to pay spousal support and lawyer fees. His wife was 42 and had not been employed during their 20 years of marriage. But Arnold demanded that his lawyer fight to avoid all payments. Of course, they could do that - the legal system works that way.

In the end, the trial court ordered Arnold to pay his wife 40% of his net income on a temporary basis, then 32% thereafter. The Court of Appeal agreed. Arnold was ordered to pay his wife's legal fees of $50,000. His own lawyer's bill was over $100,000. Arnold was angry and devastated - yet he was the one who had insisted on fighting a battle that he couldn't possibly win.

Barbara and her husband had lived for years on her inheritance.

When she first received it, she combined her funds with those in a joint account and put stocks in both names. She bought a house and put her husband's name on it. In order to avoid embarrassing him, she repeatedly told their acquaintances that all their money came from her husband's successful business (although it actually had failed).

Barbara's lawyers told her that there was no way she could get all her inheritance back, in fact probably not any of it. But she demanded that they try. So they tried. The legal system allows presentation of two points of view, no matter how unlikely one is to win. Barbara's legal and accounting fees added up to more than $50,000. Yet all the courts they asked said she had commingled and transmuted her separate property into community property. (We will translate those terms later.) What was left of Barbara's fortune was divided between her and her husband. She herself had insisted on a futile, expensive battle.

Chuck held the purse strings and kept the family books. His lawyer told him many documents were needed to handle his case, such as all credit card bills, the deed to his house, copies of his pay stubs, pension information, bank statements, pink slips, and tax returns. The lawyer asked him for those documents a dozen or more times. Chuck always said his priorities were elsewhere.

Chuck's wife's lawyer took his deposition, and when Chuck did not deliver the requested documents, the judge ordered him to produce them. Only when a substantial fine and a possible jail sentence appeared imminent did Chuck cooperate. Chuck's lawyer billed him over $10,000 just for dealing with the document production issue. Misplaced priorities cost Chuck plenty.

What do the cases of Arnold, Barbara, and Chuck tell us?

First, divorce is so unpleasant that we may try to ignore it. Like the ostrich with its head in the sand, we believe that reality will disappear if we don't look at it. But refusal to face the facts of divorce law and ignoring the required tasks can make the experience much worse, as well as more costly.

Second, we see that Arnold, Barbara, and Chuck all needed more knowledge about the divorce process. If they had known more in the beginning or acquired some understanding as they went along, they would not have incurred such high fees. Their knowledge would also have helped them achieve a more satisfactory result.

Third, spouses reach the decision to divorce at very different times. Divorce is a shattering personal experience – especially to the partner who wants to stay married. Perhaps Arnold's, Barbara's, and Chuck's spouses had been unhappy and contemplated divorce for years. They (the spouses) had moved through the adjustment process and were anxious to get on with their lives. Arnold, Barbara, and Chuck needed to go through that process too, but first they had to acknowledge their losses. These losses included social status, fair treatment, companionship, shared parenting, expectations about the future, lifestyle, and even personal identity. Each would have been far better off in the long run to deal with their misfortune through counseling, rather than fighting a losing battle with the legal system.[1]

Who is this book for?

This book is for you if you are thinking about dissolving your marriage or if you are in the midst of a divorce. It can help orient you in a field of terribly complex law and procedure. Especially in Family Law, the lawyer and client must work as a team to be effective. This book is designed to help you be a better team player.

It's also for a wider range of people, such as those who have friends or relatives in the midst of a divorce. Why? Because divorce can leave them so emotionally distraught that they can't cooperate with their own lawyers. You can give them more support if you are knowledgeable about the divorce process.

If you are a social worker, therapist, psychologist, or minister who counsels people involved in divorce, you can do a better job if you have some understanding of the legal process. This book is for you, too.

---

[1] See:Diane Vaughn, *Uncoupling: Turning Points in Intimate Relationships,* Vintage Books, New York, 1990.

CALIFORNIA DIVORCE

What does this book cover?

You'll find here the general legal rules and procedures that control the dissolution of marriage. The information makes no pretense of being scholarly or a complete legal reference. Nor does it constitute legal advice for your particular situation. Family Law is a very complex business, all of which cannot be contained in any single book. Every case presents a different set of circumstances, and no "cookbook" could apply to every stew. You need a lawyer to advise you exactly how the law and the facts of your situation fit together.

Part I deals with what lawyers call "procedural law." The term defines itself - how the law proceeds. And it proceeds so formally that procedure is often more important than substance. Most of Part I will apply to your case, so you should start from the beginning and read through this section.

Part II deals with "substantive law," the substance of the law. You can skim through this section to find the parts that are relevant for you.

On page 99 you will find endnotes with references for the legal cases mentioned. Following these are four appendices with forms to help you prepare information for a lawyer who will handle a divorce and samples of settlement figures.

Everything you learn from this book about the procedure and substance of California divorce law will reduce the likelihood of an expensive education in court.

Part I

<u>Procedure And You</u>

CALIFORNIA DIVORCE

I. What Is "Law"?

If you want to understand divorce and Family Law, you need to know how laws are made in the United States. Laws are made by the Congress and state Legislature and are called "Statutes," "Acts," or "Bills." A whole set of Acts is called a "Code." Law also is created by decisions of the appellate courts, such as the Courts of Appeal or the Supreme Court.

In this book we refer to a set of enactments in the California Family Code called the "Family Law Act,"[1] which dates from the Family Law Act passed back in 1969. Although amended over and over, the whole group of Code Sections is still referred to as "The Family Law Act," and can be found in a public law library under the California Family Code. If you want to look at the Family Law Act, or read about cases that might apply to you, you can go to the law library at your county courthouse.

Court decisions which are "laws" - in Family Law or in any other field of law - are created through the appellate process as follows: First, your case is heard in Superior Court. If the decision after your trial is not satisfactory to you, and if your dissatisfaction arises because you think the judge misapplied the law to the facts of your case, you can, as a matter of right, appeal to the Court of Appeal for the district in which your trial court is located. If you don't like the decision of the Court of Appeal, under limited circumstances, you can appeal to the California Supreme Court. Under even more limited circumstances you might be able to appeal to the United States Supreme Court. The decisions of these courts form "Law" or the legal basis for later decisions by judges.

The various decisions of Appellate or Supreme Courts are found in law libraries under Courts' Decisions. You will find references to case Names and then numbers. Every time a case number is cited, the first number is the number of the volume. For example, "10 Cal. 4th 1100" means Volume 10 of the fourth series of California Supreme Court. Reports at page 1100. "27 Cal.App. 4th 555" means Volume 27 of the fourth series of the reports of the California Appellate Courts and the page number 555.

Whether you want a dissolution of marriage, a legal separation, or a decision concerning your children without divorce or legal separation, this is the system that you will be in. If you and your spouse can communicate, you may want to attempt some form of alternative resolution rather than going to court. There are various approaches that can be used to resolve conflicts without confrontation. There are variations in how you use the system, but only the court can terminate your legal marital status.

Your first decision will be whether to seek your own lawyer or try to "do it yourself." Let's talk first about whether to hire a lawyer.

II. Different Paths to Divorce

A. Can I do it myself?

Yes, certain "Divorce Centers" will process your papers if you and your spouse have reached an agreement. But, you run a high risk of losing valuable assets, putting your future at considerable risk, or creating a long-lasting legal problem. This concept is called "missing issues." "Issues" are different types of problems, rights, assets and liabilities. Every kind of legal point that should be resolved is lumped under the word "issue." Issues are not just something to argue about - an issue is something very real that could involve a great deal of money if it is not considered and resolved. So you might easily miss issues if you do not at least consult with an experienced Family Law lawyer. Here are some examples:

Connie had acquired no skills during her 20-year marriage to help her become employable. While she wanted very much to stand on her own after her divorce, five years and several illnesses later she was unable to do so. In "doing it herself," she did not provide for a "retention of jurisdiction" on the issue of spousal support. If she had, she would have been able to go back for more help from her former husband. Instead, she had to turn to public agencies for her basic needs.

Jack was anxious to help Louise get on her feet and turned the entire family business over to her. She loved the business, but did not have a good track record of making it profitable. In their do-it-yourself divorce they provided that Louise get the house and the business. Jack did not have a lawyer to advise him that if the business failed, he was still responsible for the lease. So when the business did fail, he was faced with a $100,000 obligation. At the time of the dissolution, he could have obtained security from Louise to compensate him for such a disaster.

Sara had enjoyed participating in Sam's military career. But Sam's assignment to a different part of the country or the world had made it impossible both for Sara to develop her own earning skills and for the two of them to acquire any assets. Sam said his military pension was "his," and Sara agreed. Later, Sara died in poverty. The division of the military pension (which was not "his" at all but was "theirs" under California law) could have saved her.

B. I understand your point. I still want to try an alternative to the adversary system. Is there something else available?

Yes. There is a process called "Alternate Dispute Resolution."

C. Tell me about it. Can I by-pass the courts altogether?

The court must approve your final agreement and grant the decree of dissolution of marriage, but reaching agreement can be handled in many different ways.

D. Do I have a choice about having a judge decide?

Yes, the majority of divorces in California are settled now without a judge's decision. Courts manage disputes as well as resolve them. Today, alternative dispute resolution (ADR) is used extensively within and outside the judicial system. ADR includes mediation, arbitration, "Special Masters," private judging, collaborative law, judicial case management and settlement conferences. These services are offered by Family Law lawyers, private mediators, and occasionally by psychologists or nonprofit organizations.

A number of ADR processes are available through the family court system in California. For example, the California Legislature mandates that child custody and visitation issues be mediated prior to being decided by a judge. You can also choose to have any or all of your other issues worked out through a mediator. In all processes, the assistance of a Family Law Lawyer is important.

E. What is mediation?

Mediation is a process for resolving disputes in which a neutral third person guides the parties to an informed, mutually satisfactory agreement. Although this might include compromising and moderating some demands, the participants often come up with creative ideas that meet the needs of each of them. Because mediation is confidential, the exchange of information and proposals is often more open. A high percentage of mediated agreements are carried out because they were developed by the parties themselves.

F. Do all mediators operate the same way?

No. Mediators have different styles of mediation. All mediators function as intermediaries who see their role as facilitating dispute resolution. Some mediators may let the two lawyers or the parties handle most of the issues. These mediators limit their roles to communicating proposals and identifying underlying interests of the parties. Other mediators are more directive and may offer proposals for settlement and make recommendations. Generally, mediators prefer to meet directly with the husband and wife who are working on their divorce, assist them in developing the best possible agreements for both, and then have them confer separately with their own lawyers.

Since the basis of any settlement should be within a range of what a court will consider a fair and equitable award, a lawyer who is experienced in the Family Law is an effective mediator. When a non-lawyer mediator is used, both parties should have their own Family Law lawyers.

G. Are mediated agreements binding?

Once agreement is reached, the mediator or the lawyers write a settlement document for clients and counsel to sign. The signed agreement is then processed in the same manner as any other settlement document, and it becomes a binding court order. Since non-lawyer mediators, such as psychologists or mental health professionals, do not have legal expertise on which to base a settlement, it is important to have the final agreement negotiated by a Family Law lawyer.

H. Does this mean that my spouse and I can find someone to help us settle our case without fighting?

Absolutely. If you choose mediation, you can be educated on the subject of divorce law by a Family Law lawyer. If you choose this lawyer as your mediator, he or she will consider your individual facts and circumstances and help you to reach your own agreement. The lawyer will act in a counseling role, instead of in a representative or litigating capacity. The mediator acts as a counselor, a facilitator, a teacher, and a coach.

Your own lawyer may also suggest taking your case to a neutral third party, either a lawyer mediator or a private mediator. You will then each have your own lawyer, but work through the mediator to find a settlement with the advice of your own lawyer.

Mediation is much less expensive and emotionally painful than litigation. It has the advantage that you are less likely to miss issues or assets (because an experienced lawyer is advising, although not representing, you). And, if you try mediation and don't like it, you haven't given away anything forever, as can happen when you try to do it yourself.

J. Why would I choose mediation?

1. You retain control of the decision-making rather than leaving it up to a judge or arbitrator.

2. You focus on the future instead of the past.

3. You conserve your resources - both time and money.

4. You reach a result similar to the one you would get in litigation, or you may "tailor make" an outcome that suits your family.

K. What's the difference between mediation and arbitration?

In mediation the parties work out their own solutions with the help of a neutral third party, the mediator. In arbitration, the arbitrator - who may be a lawyer, a private judge, or even a financial expert - listens to both sides and delivers a decision. Arbitration may be either non-binding or binding.

L. When is mediation not a good idea?

Mediation is inappropriate when one of the parties is out to "get" the other, is distraught to the point of being unable to think clearly, or is only interested in delaying the process. Mediation works when both parties are mature, non-vindictive, and simply want to get on with their new lives.

M. What is "Collaborative Law?"

When the two lawyers agree that they will not oppose each other but cooperate to reach a fair settlement, it is called Collaborative Law. The advantages of this approach are that direct negotiations and full disclosure make the process quicker, less adversarial, and may involve lower charges by the lawyers. In most cases the lawyers using Collaborative Law sign a prior agreement not to take the case to court. It is similar to mediation. Where in mediation there is one mediator and perhaps two lawyers, in Collaborative Law both lawyers take on both the representative functions and the mediation functions.

N. Are there disadvantages to Collaborative Law?

The same disadvantages apply to Collaborative Law as to mediation - or perhaps more so. If you want the divorce right away, but your spouse is still talking about reconciliation, you are probably better off with the traditional system if it moves fairly rapidly in your county. There is room for delay in both mediation and collaborative law.

O. What does "Private Judging" mean?

Just what it sounds like. In cases where either assets or issues are complex, the public judicial system can sometimes be inadequate. It may take too long to get the case to trial, the judge may be unwilling to spend the necessary time to resolve a complicated case, or recent changes to the Criminal Justice system may have crowded out Civil and Family Law cases. Whatever the reason, many Family Law lawyers and clients have elected to by-pass the judicial system and have their issues decided privately.

P. But doesn't that just cost too much money?

It *is* expensive. Most private judges charge their regular hourly rate, which may be $200 or more in small cities and up to $350 in metropolitan areas. On the other hand, if you and your spouse, both of your lawyers, and perhaps your expert witnesses appear for trial several times, only to be told to "go away" (see section VIII in this part) you can incur many thousands of dollars in fees and costs each time. The security of knowing that your case will be heard when it is scheduled (in private judging), that you will not have to prepare for trial several times, and that you know who the judge is – may be worth the extra cost up front and could cost less in the long run.

CALIFORNIA DIVORCE

III. Lawyers and their Functions

A. Well, I think I want my own lawyer: What can he/she do for me?

Good question. The lawyer knows substantive and procedural law, and knows how to combine law and procedure with the facts and circumstances of your situation. The lawyer will tell you what is important and what is not, what you can and cannot do, how to set priorities in your case, and how to maximize your position after the divorce. If you are very emotional - as are most persons going through divorce - your lawyer will help keep you from making mistakes based on your anger or unhappiness. Your lawyer is critical to the outcome of your divorce, so it is very important to make the selection carefully.

B. What qualifications are required of a lawyer?

There are a number of general qualifications: A lawyer must generally have seven years of higher education (four years of college and three of law school). In addition, before a law school graduate can practice, he/she must pass the Bar examination - an exhaustive three-day exam on all the subjects covered in law school. About half of those who take it pass the test the first time.

C. Are there special qualifications for Family Law Lawyers?

Yes, the California State Bar certifies Family Law Specialists. They must have passed an examination in addition to the Bar, completed certain litigation procedures, and participated in advanced Family Law courses. You can get a list of Certified Specialists in your area by calling the State Bar of California (listed in your phone book in the state government section). If you pick a Certified Specialist, you are going to find someone interested in the subject, who has relevant, in-depth knowledge and has handled Family Law cases.

D. How do I shop for a lawyer?

Other lawyers often know or can find out who is good at Family Law. Friends and fellow workers are good sources of opinions of satisfied and dissatisfied clients. If you know a judge, he/she may be a good referral source, or will know where to get that information. Although some lawyers give a free half hour preliminary interview, it is worthwhile interviewing more than one lawyer, even if you have to pay a fee. Before you make a final selection, see at least two Family Law lawyers and ask some (or all) of the following questions:

1. Is a client best served by litigation, mediation, or another type of settlement? (Generally, unless your spouse is totally unreasonable, you are better off avoiding litigation.)

2. Given the facts of my case, what is the probable outcome? (After you have heard several answers, you will be able to evaluate the lawyer.)

3. Are there problem areas in my case which would cause higher fees than normal? What are they?

4. If one of us runs a small business, what will it cost to appraise it?

5. What do you charge? (Unless you get a clear answer, go elsewhere.)

6. My spouse has threatened to "hide money," "not pay a dime," or "take me for everything." Describe your own situation. Ask, "How would you handle this problem?" (The answers will help you pick the right lawyer.)

7. How do you run your office?

8. Do you use paralegals/legal assistants? (If so, the total fee for your case could be less. Paralegals are billed at a substantially lower hourly rate than are lawyers.)

9. Will you or an associate handle my case? What is expected of me? How much will I be consulted? Can I call you at home? (Stay away from a "yes" answer to that last question - it may mean the lawyer isn't very busy.)

10. I'm shopping for a lawyer; who besides you is a good Family Law lawyer? (If the same name keeps coming up that is a positive sign.)

11. How much attention do you pay to details? (You don't want anyone on the extreme end of this question. The over-detailed will charge too much; the under-detailed will get you into trouble.)

12. What do you think of the local judges? (Stay away from a negative answer - the judges may not like the lawyer either.)

13. Professional Qualifications:

   a) Are you a Certified Family Law Specialist?

   b) Are you a member of the State Bar Family Law Section?

   c) Are you a member of the local bar Family Law Section?

   d) Do you like Family Law work?

14. Do you see any problems in our working together? If so what would they be?

E. Are there questions that I shouldn't ask?

You bet. Many inexperienced lawyer shoppers ask questions that simply will not produce an answer that you can evaluate. For example, don't ask:

1. Are you aggressive?

2. Can you guarantee a quick settlement?

3. How can I cheat my spouse out of getting anything from me?

F. What is my personal response to the lawyer?

This is probably the most important question to ask yourself after the interviews. Remember, you and your lawyer need to work as a team. No matter how good everything else looks, if you don't like him/her, you won't have a good outcome. Or at least, you won't *think* you had a good outcome. So pick somebody you like.

G. How much will it cost?

Fees: These are what the lawyer gets to earn his/her living. They can be hourly, in a lump sum or fixed fee, or contingent. Almost all Family Law lawyers charge by the hour. So if you want to talk all day on the telephone to your lawyer, be prepared for a large bill. (Yes, telephone calls are charged; the lawyer is spending professional time talking to you.)

Costs: These include every type of expense incurred through the legal process, except the fees that represent the lawyer's own work. For example, court filing fees, appraisal fees, court reporter's fees, accountant's fees and also telephone, fax, and copying charges are passed on to the client. In a complex case the costs may exceed the lawyer's fees. One of the things that you might ask your lawyer about before hiring him/her is, "What do you include under the heading of costs that are charged separately from your fees?"

Retainer: This is a lump sum, like a deposit, which usually ranges from $500 up. An average retainer is about $4,000. If child custody is involved, it may be substantially higher. There are geographical variations. Retainers are usually much higher in central metropolitan areas. Retainers are charged in advance, and the hourly rate is usually billed against the retainer.

Paralegals/Legal Assistants: Much routine work in many offices can be delegated to a skilled non-lawyer and billed at a much lower hourly rate. If your lawyer doesn't use legal assistants, your bill probably will be higher.

H. Who pays the fees and costs?

You do. If you have no money, but your spouse does, he/she may be ordered to contribute to your fees. But don't count on it. And whoever "wants" the divorce has nothing to do with it.

J. How can I reduce the total costs and fees?

That's what this book is about. Here are a few suggestions:

1. Evaluate why your fees may be higher or lower than average. This is a complex question. You may have more complicated assets than the average couple, or difficult issues regarding child custody or support. It may be that your spouse or the other lawyer is

unreasonable - or even that you, yourself, are wanting something unrealistic. But higher fees should be evaluated throughout the case. On the other hand, low fees may mean a sloppy job, missed assets, or lack of communication with you about your case.

2. Cooperate with your lawyer. You can do much of the paralegal work yourself. For example, if you have a number of bank accounts, IRA's, and other such assets, you should carefully gather the most recent statement regarding each asset, and the statement closest to your date of separation and organize these in a book with index tabs. If your lawyer wants to look at a pattern of spending, volunteer to analyze bank account deposits, checks, etc., under the lawyer's direction. Being your own paralegal can help save thousands of dollars. On the other hand, don't give your lawyer every piece of paper that has ever passed through your hands. The proper balance is important.

3. Use the lawyer's time sparingly. You may be getting divorced because your wife lost your grandmother's diamond ring, smashed your car, or has a general attitude of disrespect for the things you try to provide for the family. You are entitled to have your marriage dissolved because you and your wife have irreconcilable differences. You are not entitled to recover the cost of the ring or the car. Don't try to do it under some other guise or blow some other issue out of proportion, such as valuation of the furniture, as you will spend more in fees than the items cost originally. There is just no point in running up a $2,000 bill in order to deal with $200 worth of furniture.

4. Don't try to use the process to "get even." Many husbands and wives are getting divorced because they didn't communicate during the marriage, or if they communicated, they had overwhelming disagreements. The law is very specific and very narrow, as we will see. If your attitude is "he owes me," you are not going to do anything except run up a big bill. You cannot address those grievances through the existing legal process. You could before 1970, but not now.

5. Consider some type of counseling or therapy during the process. If Arnold, Barbara and Chuck, whose stories were told in the

introduction to this book, had been able to work through their disappointments, anger and grief over the end of their marriages, they would have been better able to focus on the legal issues, and not the emotional ones. Their fees would have been substantially less.

K. You have convinced me to be reasonable. What happens if my spouse is not? What happens if my spouse hires a "hard-hitting" aggressive, unreasonable lawyer?

If that happens to you, it is similar to being on a roller coaster you do not like. You must hang on and ride it out. Most cases eventually end. But here are some suggestions:

1. Ask your lawyer to find out what your spouse and his/her lawyer want. If you think their position is unreasonable, ask your lawyer if the cost to you in challenging your spouse's position exceeds the potential benefit of a court fight. If it does, you do not want to fight. Consider the "cost-benefit ratio." Always evaluate your lawyer's recommendations with this principle in mind.

2. Try early and often to reach a settlement. An old adage in business is, "The worst settlement is better than the best you can do in court." That isn't completely true in Family Law, but you need to remember it when you think about settlement proposals.

3. If the opposing lawyer will not present a settlement offer saying, "I don't know anything about this case," bend over backwards to get them the information they request.

4. If the opposing lawyer is "too busy" to deal with your lawyer's requests, ask your lawyer to set the case for trial (See section VIII in this part) and wait for the settlement conferences to discuss your matter. Many lawyers really are too busy to do anything but handle their court appearances. It is rare that waiting makes things worse. Sometimes the passage of time mellows a combative spouse.

IV. Emergencies and Restraining Orders

A. What do I do if there is an emergency? My spouse came at me with a knife and I barely escaped. Or: My spouse is spending all our money and has threatened to take the children and disappear.

Your situation is not unusual. Many divorces start with an emergency. Couples who have lived peacefully together for years do and say the most awful things to each other as the marriage crumbles. If they don't go at each other with knives, they may hit each other or threaten to do so. Or there can be a veiled threat such as "you better watch out," or "I'm going to get you," or "you'll never see the children again," or something similarly ominous. Because this type of behavior is so common, we have devoted this entire chapter to Restraining Orders.[2]

B. Tell Me About Restraining Orders:

Let's look at the first category: Automatic Temporary Restraining Orders or "ATRO." They apply to the Petitioner upon filing the petition, and to the Respondent on service[3]. The orders remain in effect during the action unless they are changed sometime in the legal process.

There are three ATRO's that take effect <u>automatically</u> at the beginning of a dissolution action. The first protects children and restrains both of you from removing your minor children from the state without written consent of the other parent or the court. If either of you do that, it could be a criminal offense. Be

21

very careful you do not file for divorce, then take the children to Lake Tahoe or Las Vegas for the weekend. You could get a $10,000 fine and end up in jail.

The second ATRO restrains use and disposal of property. Usually you can use your property for ordinary living expenses - but not tickets to Paris. When the action is filed and served, both of you are restrained from "transferring, encumbering, hypothecating, concealing, or in any way disposing of any property, real or personal," without the other party's written consent or a court order . . . " except for usual business expenses or necessities of life. "Necessities of life" include lawyer's fees to pursue your action. Violation of these restraining orders may mean that the property "wasted" will be awarded to the offending party as part of his or her eventual share. The effect of that is that the "wasting party" wastes only his or her property - not yours.

The third ATRO restrains you and your spouse from changing anything about any existing insurance policies. The ATRO's are not exclusive. Either of you may ask the Court to change them, terminate them or make additional restraining orders.

C. What other types of restraining orders are there?

Almost every type of uncivilized conduct can be restrained. That includes physical assault, threats of physical assault, and other so-called "domestic violence." Not only can your spouse be restrained from this type of conduct, but he/she can be removed from the family residence.

D. What do I have to do to get these restraining orders? I have to work and can't do so when my spouse keeps yelling at me about what an awful person I am.

Protective Orders may be granted *ex parte* (literally, without a party) on an emergency and temporary basis until the time of the hearing 20 to 25 days later. They then expire unless the court reissues them at the hearing. To obtain a restraining order, you must prepare a detailed statement, under penalty of perjury, (called a "declaration") of why you need the order and what your spouse has done to justify being restrained. A typical conduct-type restraining order enjoins a party from contacting, molesting, attacking, striking, stalking, threatening, sexually assaulting, battering, harassing, telephoning, destroying personal property, or disturbing the peace of the other party.

E. **My spouse should not be conducting himself/herself in this uncivilized manner. I don't think a court order telling him/her not to do what he/she already knows is improper will help. How do I get the person out of the house?**

You must present the Court with a Declaration showing that you have a right to possession of the house, that he/she has assaulted or threatened to assault you, and that his/her remaining in the house would result in physical or emotional harm to you. In other words, if your spouse recently came at you with a knife, you can probably get an immediate *ex parte* exclusion order. If your spouse has done nothing so dramatic, you must wait until the time of the hearing, where you need only show that physical or emotional harm would otherwise result.

F. I am still very uncomfortable about this. Can you guarantee that no harm will come to me or the children if I get a restraining order?

Absolutely not! The Court can make the order, but the judge will not be there to be sure your spouse complies with it. If you fear for your safety or your life, simply move out of the house yourself, at least on a temporary basis to allow the situation to cool off. Your doing so will not affect your property rights nor be considered abandonment of the residence. However, it may affect your right to custody of the children if you leave them.

G. I agreed to what was called a "mutual restraining order," even though I hadn't done anything wrong. Then I tried to buy a gun and was turned down. What happened?

You shouldn't agree to a Mutual Restraining Order. Each person who wants/needs a restraining order must have an independent basis to get it and must make an independent request. Once domestic violence restraining orders are granted against you, even if by agreement, you are prohibited from ownership or possession of firearms for so long as the order is in effect.

H. We were never married. Can I still get restraining orders?

Yes. The Domestic Violence Prevention Act is intended to remedy "abuse" between cohabitants, former cohabitants, in dating relationships, between parents of children, relatives, or other victims of "abuse" in a specified "domestic" setting. You can get them both *ex parte* and at the scheduled hearing.

J. Is it really as strict as that sounds?

Both laws and enforcement are designed to keep people from injuring each other in their homes. It's the best protection we have.

V. Getting Started on a Divorce

A. What does separation mean?

You are "separated" in the legal sense when you or your spouse has come to the conclusion that your marriage has irreconcilably broken down. Often, but not always, that will be demonstrated by one person's moving out of the house or into a different bedroom. Separation is not the same thing as "Legal Separation" which is described in Part II, Section I. Litigation over date of separation also generates substantial fees and costs just to straighten out what is community property and what is separate.

1. Why is separation important?

Under Family Code 771 (discussed in Part II) all of your earnings are your separate property after separation. That could make an enormous difference in your financial settlement.

2. If I move out of the house, am I separated?

Not necessarily. In the case of *In Re Marriage of Baragry* [4] Dr. Baragry moved out of the house and onto his boat with his secretary. He continued to come home with his dirty laundry for his wife to do. He sent her birthday and anniversary gifts and took her to various Medical Association functions. He claimed his separation was the date that he moved out of the house. She claimed that it was several years later -- the date she filed for the dissolution. The Court of Appeal agreed with her - and said that most of the incidents of marriage continued to be present, and also that he who leads a polygamous lifestyle must bear its financial burdens.

B. What should I do before the first interview with my lawyer.

Even if there is an emergency, you will still have to start with an initial interview with your lawyer. Before you have the first interview with a prospective lawyer, fill out the information sheets in Appendix A. If it is an emergency, obviously you cannot do this until later. However, the more information that can be provided to the lawyer at the early stages, the less your divorce is going to cost.

C. What papers are required?

The action starts off with a number of pieces of paper. The first and most important is the "Petition for Dissolution of Marriage." In the Petition you ask for various relief, such as division of community property, spousal support, custody and child support. If you have requested emergency (*ex parte*) relief, the court will make those orders, coupled with a notice of the date for a hearing. Also included in those papers will be a Summons notifying your spouse of the action. The majority of the papers are designed by the Judicial Council and are on preprinted forms that look deceptively simple. They are not! If the wrong box is checked, serious problems can occur later.

Both of you must submit to the court a "Preliminary Declaration of Disclosure" within 60 days of service of the Petition. The disclosures include an Income and Expense Declaration and a Schedule of Assets and Debts. The "Final Declaration of Disclosure" (unless waived) is due from both parties before or at the time of entering into a property or support settlement agreement and, in any event, no later than 45 days before the first assigned trial date.

D. Where is the action filed?

The action will be filed in the Superior Court in the county of your residence or that of your spouse. To file for Dissolution of Marriage, you or your spouse must have been a resident of the county for at least three months and the state of California for six months. There are no residence requirements for a Legal Separation.

E. My spouse moved out several months ago into an adjoining county. Does it make any difference where I file?

It makes an enormous difference. Talk to lawyers from both counties and outline your situation. The courts - particularly the court where emergency matters are heard - may deal with your case differently from one county to the next. Sometimes, the Family Law Judge in one county will announce that he/she sees things a certain way and the Family Law Judge in the adjoining county makes a contrary announcement. So where you elect to file can be significant.

F. After the papers are completed, what happens then?

One of the most basic elements of American law is that nobody's rights can be taken away without notifying that person and providing an opportunity to be heard. In Family Law this process is accomplished by "service" of the Summons and Petition (your papers starting the case) on the other party. The papers served also give the other person a notice of the first hearing and of any restraining orders which you have obtained *ex parte* and that you are seeking to have made permanent. Unless there is service according to the rules, orders of the court are meaningless and cannot be enforced. In fact, the legal words used are "the court lacks jurisdiction."

When you first go to see your lawyer, bring a picture of your spouse and a written description of his/her automobile, including the color, model, year and license plate. This will make the service of the papers simpler and cheaper, and get the case off to a solid start.

G. How can service be made?

In California, service can be accomplished in a number of ways. The most common is personal service, that is, a process server will simply hand you the papers. If that doesn't work, he/she can leave copies at your home with a responsible person and mail you additional copies. Within California you can accept service by acknowledging it in writing, by signing an "Acknowledgement of Receipt." Outside California you may be served by mail with a return receipt requested. This means that picking up the papers at the post office and signing the return receipt constitutes valid service.

If you are about to be served, don't deny who you are, run and hide, or refuse to answer the door. The process server will put the papers in your car, under the door, or on the floor. *That* is valid service. Rarely is it worth trying to avoid service - it merely increases the bill that you yourself may be required to pay.

VI. First Court Hearing

A. Why is there a first court hearing? Is that the trial?

No. The first hearing is not usually the trial of your case. It is the hearing at which the court has the opportunity to preserve a status quo as much as possible after the time of the initial breakup, but before the marriage is actually dissolved. It is usually necessary to determine what happens to the children and how the finances will be handled in the interim. If you have asked for any emergency (*ex parte*) relief, such as a residence exclusion order, the matter must be set for a hearing, and your spouse has an opportunity to be heard.

This first court hearing is often called the hearing on the "Order to Show Cause." It usually occurs about a month after the papers are served. Orders issued by the court after this hearing are called *Pendente Lite* orders, or merely Temporary Orders.

B. What will happen to the children?

If you and your spouse disagree about custody of your children, the first step will be mediation. You will first go to a department usually known as the "Family Court Services" and discuss your situation with a skilled court mediator. In Los Angeles this process is called "Conciliation Court." The mediator will try to get you to work out a temporary arrangement regarding custody. If you and your spouse can't agree, then the judge will make the decision - but not until all efforts to try to resolve the matter voluntarily have failed. Your children are much better served if you decide how they will be cared for - rather than if a stranger decides.

C. I'm scared. I have no money. What will happen to me?

Preservation of the status quo means dividing up existing salaries and income like dividing a pie. If you or your spouse has requested child or spousal support, at the first hearing the judge will make an order for support. That support will be based on guideline schedules in use in most California counties. The numbers are quite complicated but the principle is simple: the court is going to divide the available income pie in an equitable fashion. Depending upon what you each earn, how many children there are and what custodial arrangements are made, you will come out of the hearing with 40% - 60% of the total.

This is one of the areas of divorce which is most emotionally painful and financially devastating. Most couples live up to or beyond their income levels. Most couples have significant debts. That income now has to stretch to accommodate two households. What is often forgotten are the debts. The court will not allow debts to be paid before support. So a good credit rating is often one of the fatalities of a dissolution of marriage.

D. Can we divide property at this first hearing?

Perhaps. Occasionally, the judge at the first hearing will divide property. For example, if foreclosure of your house is threatened, the court has the authority to order it sold prior to trial. This authority is rarely exercised. Property is generally divided later, at trial or by property settlement agreement.

E. I'd like to know more about this process before it happens to me. Can I do that?

Absolutely. It is an excellent idea to get comfortable with the legal process before it happens to you. You can do this by spending one or two mornings in court. Go to the county courthouse and ask the clerk for the "Family Law" or "Domestic Relations" Department. If you are uncertain about which county to use, go to the Family Law Department in both counties. No matter how detailed a description this book might give you, or what your lawyer might tell you about what happens in court, there is no substitute for viewing it personally. If "one picture is worth a thousand words," one visit is worth a thousand pictures. And you can do it as often as you like. You will find it very educational.

VII. Discovery

A. What is discovery?

"Discovery" is what makes real-life practice of law different from television dramas. Nothing in the law happens suddenly, and very little happens by surprise. Your lawyer has the right to ask your spouse about everything related to the case. That means just about everything in the area of finances and issues related to custody of your children. Included in discovery are subpoenas, interrogatories, requests for production of documents, and depositions.

B. It sounds expensive. Before the process starts, what can I do to cut costs?

Quite a lot. Sometimes one of the spouses will monopolize the financial information of the parties and the other spouse will know little or nothing about their assets and liabilities. However, it is far more common that each spouse has substantial knowledge. Since a major portion of the lawyer's job is to collect and marshal information, your lawyer's time is best (and most economically) spent when you provide your lawyer with every bit of relevant information you can.

Go back and look at Appendix A. If you have not provided your lawyer with *detailed* information before the first court hearing, it is important to do so immediately. <u>There is no other area where you can save as much money as by following these instructions.</u>

C. All right, I've done that, now how do we find out about the things I want to know about my spouse?

Competent counsel will generally exchange information voluntarily or upon request. This method is far less expensive than is formal discovery. Your lawyer will simply prepare a list of documents that are important and ask the other lawyer for them. Be prepared to have your spouse's lawyer ask you for a multitude of documents also. Be sure to cooperate in this request. It will save money.

D. We did that and he/she said something rude and refused to supply the information. What do we do now?

Okay. Now we must use formal methods of discovery. Let's see what they are.

1. **Interrogatories:** Either of you may send the other formal written questions which must be answered under oath within 30 days of their service. These questions are called "interrogatories," and are an inexpensive method of gaining information and narrowing issues. In Family Law, you should probably start with a first set of standard or "form" interrogatories. If interrogatories are served on you and you don't respond, your spouse can obtain a court order to force you to do so. This is expensive and a foolish waste of money, so make sure you and your lawyer answer the questions completely.

2. **Requests for Production of Documents:** Either of you can ask the other to produce any and all documents having anything to do with the dissolution and its related matters. That is anything to do with support, community property, separate property, the children, or any other matter that can be decided by the court. The formal method of requesting documents is not a great deal different from the informal method. But, as with interrogatories, if there is no response, it can lead to court orders, sanctions, possible jail time and a big waste of money.

E. This sounds all right, but what I really want to do is have my lawyer talk to my spouse. Can we do that?

Yes. By far the most common type of discovery does just that. It is called a "deposition." A deposition is a duplication of a court proceeding without a judge. Your lawyer may ask questions of your spouse (and your spouse's lawyer can ask you questions) in a setting in which the questions and answers are recorded by a certified shorthand reporter and later bound into a permanent volume.

Depositions have several functions. First, they narrow the issues so that your lawyer can find out exactly your spouse's position on various matters. For example, if you and your spouse agree that your grandmother's furniture is your separate property, that issue can be eliminated. If not, and you are trying to preserve that furniture as your separate property, your lawyer must ask your spouse the basis of his/her opinion: If there are any receipts to prove the furniture is community, when he/she first saw the furniture, if the two of you ever had any conversations concerning the status of the furniture, and many other questions. By eliminating issues in this way you are "narrowing the issues which need to be resolved by the court." Narrowing issues saves money!

Second, depositions tend to "freeze" testimony. That is - if a party testifies one way at a deposition, and another way at trial, it is unlikely that the judge will believe anything the person says. So each spouse is "stuck" with his/her deposition testimony. Third, a deposition is very useful in helping the lawyer determine how effective your spouse is likely to be in court. And, finally, if the assets, liabilities and income are very complex, a deposition is essential to educate the lawyers.

F. I need to know more about taking my spouse's deposition.

1. What if your spouse won't answer the question?

Your lawyer will ask the court reporter to "certify" the question, and then ask the judge to order him/her to answer. If the judge makes that order and if your spouse still refuses to answer, there are many remedies. A fine or jail sentence is possible, but what is most effective is to "strike the pleadings" of the other spouse. Then he/she has no rights before the court.

2. What if he/she is lying?

If you can prove it, that is clearly to your advantage. In fact, if you can prove that only part of his/her testimony is not truthful, you are probably going to be the prevailing party on contested issues. Many people lie and cheat in the world, but they are generally unsuccessful in getting the court system to help them. Judges are quite experienced in judging a person's credibility and often know when witnesses are lying. The foundation of our legal system assumes that people tell the truth when they come to court, so judges react very negatively to witnesses who lie.

CALIFORNIA DIVORCE

3. Can I be present?

Of course. It is your case. You always have the right to be present at your spouse's deposition and should plan to do so, unless your lawyer advises you that it would be counterproductive.

G. Will I have to have my deposition taken?

Yes, if your spouse's lawyer wants to take your deposition.

H. Can you give me some instructions about how best to handle it. I think it's going to be an ordeal.

It is. But let's look at how to do the best job. There are several instructions that most lawyers give to their clients:

1. Tell the truth. You must – you are under oath. However do not depreciate yourself. For example, if you genuinely believe that you are unable to work long hours of overtime, then the answer "Yes" to the question, "You really are able to work overtime, aren't you?" would not be the truth.

2. Don't guess. If you don't know the answer or if you can't remember, say so! Nobody is going to think you are stupid if you can't remember something. Most of us can remember only life milestones, not day-to-day trivia. The deposition "freezes" your testimony, so a wrong guess can be disastrous.

3. Answer only the question: don't run on at the mouth. A deposition is very expensive! Extra words create extra expense. If you can answer a question with ten words, do not use one hundred. However, you are not limited to a "yes" or "no" answer.

4. Don't volunteer information. You are not obligated to do so, and if you do, it could be damaging to your case. Just wait for the question, answer the question, and then wait for another question.

5. Don't try to convince the other side of the merit of your case. You won't be able to do it, and you will find yourself caught in a web. Besides, it really doesn't matter whether the other side likes you or not. You can never help yourself at the deposition, but you can hurt your case.

I. Can my mother/friend/therapist be present?

The law in this area is not clear. However, most lawyers will allow other persons to be present if the request is reasonable and if there is enough space in the room. This is especially true with your own deposition as opposed to your spouse's deposition.

J. Can I find out about anything from persons other than my spouse?

Yes, sometimes third parties will voluntarily provide requested information. This is especially true if they will receive money if they cooperate. For example, if your lawyer is an escrow holder of funds for payment of bills, the creditors will almost always respond to a request for a copy of their bill.

If they will not provide information upon request, documents and other matters must be obtained from third parties by subpoena. In addition, your lawyer can take the deposition of any third party (about relevant matters) through the subpoena process.

CALIFORNIA DIVORCE

VIII. Preparing For Settlement and/or Trial

A. We have been at this for more than six months now and there seems to be no end in sight. I've met someone else and want to remarry. When can I do it?

You can be divorced, even if you haven't settled the property or support, by a process called "bifurcation." Bifurcation is a procedure whereby all of the other issues (support, property division - even custody), are separated out or "bifurcated" from the status of the marriage. The judge dissolves the marriage before deciding the other issues.

There are a number of restrictions which the court may impose on you as a condition of the bifurcation. You may have to provide tax liability indemnification, continued health insurance coverage, indemnification regarding some probate matters, pension and social security benefits as well as anything else the court thinks is reasonable. Some of the conditions could turn out to be very expensive. You may be better off not to bifurcate and to wait to resolve all the issues at the same time.

B. But I have been trying resolve the rest of the issues for months. He/she refuses. What can I do?

Generally one party wants the divorce. The other party either does not want it, is not sure that he/she wants it, or just wants to use the legal process to fight. For that reason, it is generally necessary for the lawyers to move the case along by requesting a trial date. When that date arrives, either you and your spouse must come to an agreement with respect to division of property, support, and custody, or the judge will make the decisions relating to these matters.

C. How do we get a trial?

Often, before your lawyer can even request a trial, he/she must file a detailed statement of issues, assets, and liabilities with the court. In some California counties, even appraisals of property must be filed before a trial can be requested. This document, known as the "Pretrial Statement," will be prepared from the information you gave your lawyer (see Appendix A), and information obtained in discovery. (Procedures and what they are called may be different in Los Angeles County.) If you have not given your lawyer all of the information previously requested, you must do so now. He/she will need it in order to get a trial date.

In addition, a "Final Declaration of Disclosure", which includes a current Income and Expense Declaration and Schedule of Assets and Debts, is due from both parties before or at the time of entering into a property or support settlement agreement and, in any event, no later than 45 days before the first assigned trial date.

D. Can the court force my spouse to a settlement?

No. But the court can help. In California, if the case is estimated to last more than one day, the court will set a date for a mandatory settlement conference after your lawyer has filed the Pretrial Statement. You and your lawyer must appear at the appointed time. Your spouse and his/her lawyer will also appear. Then the two lawyers will go talk to the settlement judge. You and your spouse must stay out in the empty court room. Many people feel scared and alone at this time. If you feel that way, go out into the hall or into the coffee shop. On the other hand, if you can stand it, it might be a good opportunity to talk to your spouse about the settlement of the issues.

1. What happens with the judge and the lawyers?

The judge will speak with both lawyers, learn as much about the case as is possible in a short time, and make suggestions about settlement. Courts cannot possibly accommodate a trial in every case in which one is requested, so the judge will do everything possible to help achieve a settlement. You are much better served with a settlement than a trial, because it is infinitely better to make a decision about your own life than it is to hand that decision to someone who doesn't even know you.

2. Can my lawyer "sell me out"?

Why would a lawyer betray a client? A lawyer does not benefit in any way from advising a client to accept a settlement which is far less than what that client would gain in litigation. An experienced local Family Law lawyer knows the parameters of what a judge will do at trial and the judge will often indicate a ruling if asked. Since most Family Law litigants are unhappy with *any* division of assets or order for support, it is easy to feel "sold out." But it rarely happens. No bribe is big enough for a lawyer to risk his/her professional reputation on a "sell-out."

3. If my lawyer comes out laughing, what does that mean?

The judge probably told a joke unrelated to your case. Don't take it personally. You want your lawyer to be liked and respected by the judges. Laughing at the judge's jokes certainly won't hurt your case and may even help. If you have any doubts about your lawyer's intentions regarding your case, ask – you have a right to be taken seriously and treated professionally.

CALIFORNIA DIVORCE

IX. Trial

A. Are we finally ready?

Maybe not. There will probably be another settlement conference, or you may have to wait for a judge. Courts "overbook" to a substantially greater degree than do airlines. This is necessary because the majority of cases which are set for trial will not go to trial, that is, will settle - and often on the day of trial. If there were a judge available for every case that was set, there would be a number of judges without anything to do, and a higher tax bill for all of us.

B. What must we bring into court?

Many lawyers will prepare a detailed trial brief to educate the judge and to clarify and argue the issues. Unlike physicians and lawyers who are highly specialized, judges often are generalists. So a trial brief can not only be a great help to the judge, but could be the basis of the judge's decision. In Los Angeles County briefs are required. If there is only one trial brief - yours - you stand an excellent chance of prevailing.

Also, you will need to bring documentary evidence. Exhibits and other documents can be almost anything - from real property deeds to reports of experts, anything which tends to prove the case. Evidence is subject to certain restrictions as provided by law. In a complex case, documentary evidence may fill several boxes.

C. How is the judge selected?

If your county has a Family Law Department, you may know who the judge will be before you get to court. Otherwise, you must go to the Department of the Presiding Judge, where all other civil cases (personal injury actions, contract actions, dog bites, and everything else but criminal matters) are assigned. Unless your lawyer has specifically challenged a judge, you can be assigned to any judge who is available.

Challenges are "for cause," or "peremptory." A challenge for cause means that the judge is related to one of the parties or has some kind of common financial interest in your case (such as owning stock in the family business). A peremptory challenge may be exercised when you or your lawyer believe the judge would be prejudiced. This can be done only once. If you believe that all judges in the county are prejudiced, for example, a judge's wife may feel that way, the proper thing to do is to try to get what is called a "change of venue" and go to another county.

D. What happens to me if there are no judges available?

You sit and wait. Maybe you do it for a few hours or a few days. Maybe the Presiding Judge will tell your lawyer that you will be "reset," that is, you will be asked to come back in a month or two. Because criminal law has become such a complex maze, the civil side often suffers because there are not enough judges to do more than keep up with the criminal load.

Another alternative is to have your matter judged privately. Recently, many Family Law lawyers have offered their services to Family Law litigants. It is expensive, because you and your spouse must pay the private judge his/her hourly rate. But it may not be as expensive as paying two lawyers to sit and wait for the public judge.

Or, while you are waiting, you might try again to settle the case. It is important to remember that submitting your case to a stranger, even one with impressive black robes called a judge, is permitting extensive government interference into your lives. It is rolling the dice. And you probably will not like the result.

Of course, if your lawyer says the offer from your spouse is totally unreasonable ("crazy, off-the-wall," or some other such description) then you have no alternative but to wait for your "day in court." On the other hand, in all but the most unusual cases, most competent lawyers will be able to give you a range of what the judge will do. You can then achieve a settlement within that range. It is much less expensive and less painful.

E. My spouse is totally unreasonable, and we were just assigned to trial. Now what happens?

The judge may ask to see the lawyers, and you will be left in the court room, alone with your spouse again. Judges never give up trying to settle cases. If all attempts at settlement fail, the trial can begin. Your lawyer may make an opening statement which will include a brief summary of the legal issues, and what the testimony will show. Perhaps, he/she will ask for a Statement of Decision. That is a detailed statement setting forth the reasons for the court's decision. This statement forms the basis for an appeal or can set forth "circumstances" for future modification proceedings. It is extremely important and should be requested.

F. I have a lot of questions about testimony:

1. Can my spouse call me as a witness?

Yes, under Evidence Code §776, you can be called as a witness for the other side, as if under cross-examination. This is scary, but it is not so bad if you know about it before it happens.

2. What if I refuse to testify?

You really cannot. You could be sent to jail, as there is no protection against "self-incrimination" in a civil matter. If you refuse to testify, the judge would simply resolve the issue or issues against you.

3. What is cross-examination?

Your spouse's lawyer has the right to ask you questions about your testimony. It is similar, but not identical to a deposition. If you are not telling the truth, your testimony is unlikely to stand up under cross-examination. If you have lied in your deposition or you lie in court, you are in big trouble.

G. What witnesses should I bring?

Witnesses fall into two categories: "expert" and "percipient." Expert witnesses include appraisers, accountants, physicians, or other professionals. Percipient witnesses include all persons who have knowledge of the facts. You must bring in all witnesses necessary to prove your case. Often in Family Law the testimony of the two spouses is exactly the opposite of each other. The Judge will then make his/her decision based upon the testimony of the independent witnesses. So independent witnesses are essential.

H. Are there alternatives to witnesses?

Certain records can be brought into court by certain types of subpoenas. Sometimes, testimony can be etched in stone by deposition on a narrow issue. Basically, however, the judge makes the decision based on listening to and evaluating the credibility of witnesses. So there really is no effective substitute for percipient witnesses.

J. How can I help my lawyer during the trial?

During your spouse's presentation, it is worthwhile for you to write down everything that your spouse and opposing witnesses say. Your lawyer will be busy objecting and may not get everything written down. However, do not give your notes to your lawyer during the trial since that is disruptive and could cause your lawyer to miss something important. Your records can be invaluable. Then, if you disagree, you can testify in opposition.

K. At the end of the trial it will all be over, isn't that true?

Not necessarily. The judge does not have to make the decision from the bench. He/she may take the case "under submission," think about it, and notify the lawyers in writing of the decision. The judge must issue the decision within 90 days in order to continue getting a paycheck.

X. After The Trial

A. We received the judge's decision and it was completely unfair to me. What can I do?

The first thing is to take a hard look at the details of the decision. Figure out what you really got and what the other person got. You just can't imagine how many times at first reading the decision looks a lot worse than it really is. Or perhaps you simply misunderstood.

Then, on the points where you think the decision is grossly unfair, study it to see how much the "unfairness" has cost you. Compare the dollar amount or value of the "unfairness" to the total amount involved in the whole case and see whether it is worthwhile to fight or whether you should accept the outcome and live with it. Also, see whether the things that are "unfair" are "modifiable" or changeable at a later date so that you may have a second chance with another judge with more favorable facts. If you and your lawyer truly believe that you should do something more, here are some moves you can make:

1. **Statement of Decision:** If your lawyer (or spouse's lawyer) asks for this, the judge will assign one of the lawyers to prepare it. Although it is a complicated document, the basic idea is to explain the judge's reasoning and conclusions. Sometimes in the process, the judges change their minds. If not, the statement will make the appellate process cleaner, clearer, and more likely to succeed.

2. **Post trial motions:** There are a number of motions which you can make after the trial. They are too technical to describe here in

detail, but some of them are called: motion for new trial [5], motion to vacate the judgment and enter a new and different judgment [6], motion for reconsideration [7], motion to set aside the judgment based upon surprise, inadvertence or excusable neglect[8]. The first three deal with something the judge may have done wrong; the latter with something that you may have done wrong. All have very short time periods during which they can be filed. So if you and your lawyer decide to take action after you get the judge's decision, you must do it immediately.

3. **Set-aside:** Finally, if the judgment was based on actual fraud, you have a little longer to seek to vacate the judgment. You must bring your motion to set aside the judgment within one year from the time you discover or should have discovered the fraud. "Fraud" under these circumstances means that the other spouse hid something from you or prevented you from presenting your case. For example, your spouse said he/she would come after you with a gun if you went to a lawyer or resisted the proceedings in any way, and then got a judgment depriving you of all of your rights. Lying within the case may or may not qualify. You have a responsibility to investigate your own case, and your lack of diligence may keep you from getting the decision set aside.

B. Well, I think I'll appeal. How does that work?

You may appeal your case based upon an error or misapplication of the law or "abuse of discretion" by the trial judge. Trial judges have broad, but not unbridled, discretion. If there was no evidence to support the decision, that would be an abuse of discretion. For example, if all the evidence showed that you and your spouse agreed that the house was your separate property - but the judge awarded it to your spouse as her separate property - that would be an abuse of discretion. You may not appeal to re-litigate the facts, or appeal because you did not like the decision.

1. Can you tell me how much an appeal will cost?

Most lawyers continue to bill on an hourly basis for the appeal. The cost will generally be over $5,000, but the cost is much more predictable than it is for the dissolution at the trial court level. Sometimes your lawyer will recommend a specialist in appellate law. This is a good idea, because the whole process is highly technical and specialized.

2. Tell me about the appeal process.

The process begins after the formal judgment (and Statement of Decision, if you have requested it) is prepared. Unless your case has been previously bifurcated (See Section VIII A), this judgment will also be the Judgment of Dissolution of your marriage. The appealing party, called "the Appellant," prepares and files a "Notice of Appeal" and asks the court reporter to prepare the transcript of the proceedings (a written document which includes everything everybody said at trial). This may take many months. After you get the transcript, your lawyer will prepare a "brief," (written statement of the law and legal arguments to support your position at the appellate level). The other lawyer prepares a responding brief.

When the Court of Appeal reaches its decision, it must do so in writing. This writing may be published in a permanent volume. The case may then be referred back to the trial court for a decision "in accord with the principles expressed in the Court of Appeal opinion." In other words, there may be another trial. The whole process is very lengthy and may take up to three years.

3. What kind of a chance do I have?

Don't get too excited about your right to appeal. Almost every person who loses a significant amount at a trial says, "let's appeal" as though an appeal were a sure solution. Most appeals cost money and lose because the rules on appeal are that the court must respect the decision of the trial judge. Even when the trial judge is wrong on the law, the Court of Appeal has to find that the error of law is so significant as to lead to a miscarriage of justice. In the end, the Court of Appeal sustains (agrees with) approximately 80% of trial judges' decisions.

On the other hand, if the trial judge was asleep, or has done something grossly unfair, you can expect a reversal. After all, bad trial court decisions are the basis of successful appeals.

CALIFORNIA DIVORCE

XI. Enforcement

In the final analysis, if a court order, judgment or other decision is to succeed, the litigants must accept it. Remember the U.S. Supreme Court school desegregation decision in *Brown v. Board of Education* in 1954? Many of those opposed to the decision said they would not abide by it; they just weren't going to do it. It took the full weight of the Executive Branch, substantial cooperation from the Legislative Branch (the Civil Rights Acts of the 1960's), the National Guard, and nearly three decades before desegregated schools became part of the American way of life.

Like the situation with desegregation, often the litigants follow the law only because the government has the power to force it on them. In the area of Family Law, government machinery to force the parties to accept the judgment is called "enforcement" and is sadly lacking. Until the 1970s it was almost nonexistent. While it is slowly improving, one of the most needed reforms in Family Law is to strengthen the existing government enforcement machinery, to get judges to make orders that back up their prior judgments, and to award lawyer's fees if it is necessary to return to court to enforce a prior order.

If your former spouse has not been paying the required support and you seek the assistance of the court to help you, you are going to be very discouraged if the judge does not enforce the prior order. You may be so discouraged that you do not want to try again. Put another way, if it costs $1,000 in lawyer fees for a court appearance to enforce $1,000 of support, you may feel that it doesn't make sense to continue trying. Generally, your feeling will not be correct. Collection of support is often just a matter of being persistent. Eventually the judge will rule in your favor.

A. Explain the enforcement machinery. How can I collect my support?

1. Wage Assignment

Wage assignments for spousal and child support are granted automatically on request and are effective 10 days after service of an order on your spouse's employer. Your support will then be withheld from your former spouse's paycheck in a fashion similar to the way taxes are withheld. This is an effective method of collecting support so long as the payor is employed. If he/she is not employed, then collecting support will be difficult, if not impossible (unless there is independent money).

2. License Suspension

Wage assignments do not work for very small businesses or professional practices, because there are no wages. Therefore the California Legislature has provided that professional licenses can be suspended for non-payment of support. Driver's licenses can also be suspended if the payor falls more than 30 days in arrears in child support payments. The potential suspension will be most effective at the time the license comes up for renewal. Even the knowledge that a license is in jeopardy is an effective tool in getting a self-employed person to pay!

3. Security Deposit

The court that makes a child support order has authority to require the payor to deposit up to one year's payments to fund an interest-bearing trust account for the child. The account acts as a continuing guarantee for payments.

4. Contempt

After a proper motion, the Court may find the non-payer in contempt of court if there is: a) a valid court order, b) your former spouse had knowledge of the order, c) the ability to pay the order, and d) his/her nonpayment was willful. This is generally a quasi-criminal procedure and the penalty can be up to five days in jail per offense (per month). Rarely is a person sent to jail on a first or second offense. Judges dislike sending people to jail, but they occasionally do it, especially if the nonpayment is at least the third offense.

Often, simply filing the motion brings about the payment of back due support. And, if the judge makes a finding of contempt (somewhat like a guilty verdict), even though this means there may be jail time ordered, the judge may "suspend the sentence" - that is, order a jail sentence and postpone it - provided that support payments are paid on time in the future.

5. Debtor's Examination

Your attorney can demand that the parent attend a hearing in court and answer questions about his/her assets and income. That information can then be used to obtain back support by execution (see below).

6. Execution

The court may issue a Writ of Execution (an order to the Sheriff to collect money) for past unpaid support. This means that your former spouse's bank account may be taken or, under certain circumstances, his/her real property sold to satisfy the judgment. This method is fine in theory, but it is expensive and full of technicalities. The law provides so many rights to the debtor and you will find yourself so caught in the intricacies of this law, that you may forget your purpose - to collect support.

7. District Attorney

The local District Attorney's Family Support Division will enforce any support order on your request. They use all these remedies, plus they are better able to locate absent parents, deal with repeat offenders, enforce support across state lines, and intercept tax refunds than you and your private lawyer. Sometimes they are polite and helpful, sometimes not. But you have a right to their services - so take advantage of them.

B. Enforcement sounds so difficult - what can I do to make it easier?

Many things. Keep a record of the payments, record your judgment, and don't *ever* say, "it's okay not to pay." Let's look at each separately.

1. Keep careful records: This must be done in an accounting format. Every month write down the following: a) amount ordered, b) amount paid, c) date of payment, and d) total amount due (known as "arrearages"). The law assumes that the payer pays, so the burden to prove he/she did not shifts to you. You meet that burden with meticulous records, kept every month. If you keep the records, even one month of nonpayment can be collected later. If you don't, the money is lost.

2. <u>Record the judgment</u>: The judgment will be filed with the county clerk. Get a certified copy and take it to the recorder's office. Ask that your judgment be recorded. This whole process will cost less than $25 and can be worth a fortune to you. When your former spouse sells a piece of real property, your past due support will be paid from the equity, if the judgment was recorded in the same county as the property. If you know that he/she is selling real property, let the title company know about the recorded judgment and how much is owed to you.

3. <u>Give no oral waivers</u>: Don't make any statements, even out of kindness, that make the other person believe that you are going to forgive the support. Postponement and cancellation of the debt are two very different things. If you say anything implying even temporary forgiveness, you could be found to have given up the unpaid support altogether. So, if your former spouse says he/she has lost his/her job, don't say, "Forget about the support." Write him/her a letter (and keep a copy in your safe deposit box) saying something like this:

Dear Jack, (Mary)

I understand you have lost your job and have asked not to pay support this month.

I won't get a lawyer to do anything about the support payments while you are unemployed. I am willing to consider that any of the support that you cannot pay during that time will be the same as a loan from me to you. I will have the right to insist that you pay me back when you are again able to do so.

If you can pay me anything while you are out of work, it is very important to me that you do pay what you can and that you start paying the full amount each month when you have a job again. I have to insist that you let me know when you get a job.

Please stay in touch. As long as I continue to know what your situation is, and as long as you do not have a job, I will not have a lawyer do anything about the arrearage.

The best of luck to you.

If you say anything else you may give up your unpaid support.

C. What about property division? Do you mean that after the judge gives me my house, I could not get it, or I could lose it?

No, what we have been talking about has been related to ongoing rights and obligations for support over an extended period of time. Judgments for division of property should be self-executing and may contain a clause that the court can continue to supervise and enforce the division of property. Even a separate lawsuit may be filed to get what was awarded to you in the decree. But more important, the lawyers consider transferring the assets to the person to whom they were awarded to be part of their job in completing the dissolution of marriage. That is <u>not</u> true with respect to ongoing support.

CALIFORNIA DIVORCE

XII. Modification

A. Can we change any parts of the decision in the future?

Yes. The legal term for that process is called "modification," which means to change the judgment or order. Property divisions are almost always non-modifiable. For example, once the judge has awarded you the house or your pension, there is nothing that the other side can do to take it away from you. The opposite is true with support and custody, which are generally open to modification in the future.

B. How do I modify a support order?

This can be done by filing a motion with the court and giving at least 15 days notice to your former spouse of your request. Usually the Family Law judge will hear your request.

C. What do I have to show to get a support order changed?

If your former spouse wants more money or you want to pay less money, it is possible to achieve your objective if you can show "changed circumstances" since the last order. "Circumstances" is anything that has to do with your or your spouse's situation: an increase or decrease in the income of either of you, receipt of an inheritance, change in health, one party's remarriage. Child support is always modifiable and spousal support generally so upon a proper showing of "changed circumstances" (unless you have agreed in your decree that it is non-modifiable).

There are many exceptions to the "changed circumstances" rule. Child support orders made before 1993, and certainly before 1985, are probably modifiable without a showing of changed circumstances. The

Legislature has been gradually becoming aware that child support awards in middle class situations were often less than welfare payments. So if you have an older order, the judge will probably increase it on request, and probably to the amount set by the California Guidelines (See Part II, section V).

Another exception to the changed circumstances rule is that once spousal support is set, it cannot be increased just because the payor has an increase in salary or income - unless the recipient can show that his/her needs were not met at the time of the original order. The principle here is that the recipient of spousal support is not entitled to support which allows an increase in his/her standard of living beyond that established in the marriage.

D. I don't know whether I want to modify the support until I know about his/her current income. How can I get that information?

You can ask. A year after the judgment, either of you may serve a request for the production of a completed current income and expense declaration by the other. You can get these forms at the County Clerk's office, and you can do it without filing a motion for change of support. It provides an excellent, inexpensive way to find out the financial status of the other party. He/she <u>must</u> produce the completed form within 30 days. And if it comes back incorrect or untruthful, the chances are good that you will be awarded lawyer fees to get it straightened out.

If you (or your lawyer) decide to file a motion to increase or decrease support, your former spouse must produce, on request, both federal and state tax returns. They are absolutely invaluable, as they provide a check against what your former spouse reported on the income and expense declaration, and show newly acquired assets. Wages, bonuses, other income, bank statements, and asset information are subject to subpoena for modification purposes just as at the original hearing. You should obtain every bit of information you can before going into court for a modification hearing.

E. What about custody? Is that modifiable?

We'll talk more about custody in Part II. Generally, custody is governed by the changed circumstance rule also. But what is paramount with children is their best interests. Custody can be changed because the children are being mistreated, one parent is unable to continue taking care of them, one parent wants to move away, or a variety of other circumstances affecting the best interests of the children.

Part II

<u>Substantive Family Law</u>

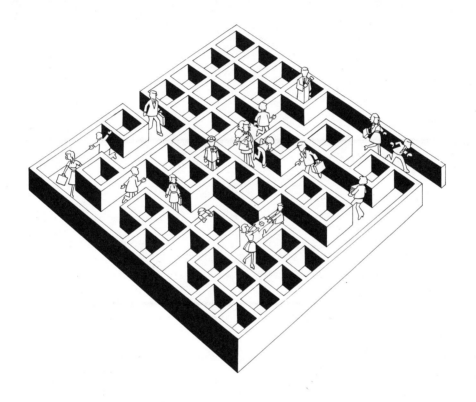

CALIFORNIA DIVORCE

I. Introduction, Definitions, and Some Miscellaneous Matters

A. Tell me about the Family Law Act in California.

The Family Law Act[1] which took effect January 1, 1970, was the first "no-fault" divorce statute in the nation. It was a drastic change in the way the law regarded divorce. Its social and economic consequences for our entire society have been far-reaching.

1. What are the grounds for dissolution of marriage?

Grounds for dissolution of marriage are "irreconcilable differences which have caused the irremediable breakdown of the marriage," and "incurable insanity."[2] Irreconcilable differences are difficult to define. The statute says they are "those grounds which are determined by the court to be substantial reasons for not continuing the marriage and which make it appear that the marriage should be dissolved." From a practical standpoint, they are simply what someone says are "irreconcilable differences."

2. Legally, how can I challenge "irreconcilable differences?"

You really cannot successfully challenge someone's testimony as to whether or not they exist. That is, as soon as your spouse says you have irreconcilable differences, and you say "no" - you have automatically created them. This area has been a major change from the old law when one person had to obtain "permission" from the other for the divorce.

3. What is legal separation?

Legal separation means that you remain married - but can have all of the other incidents of divorce. It is rarely used. As soon as one party files for a legal separation and asks for support, the other party usually asks to dissolve the marriage. Note that "separation" (see Part I, Section V.A.) is not the same as "legal separation," which is a formal legal process similar to divorce.

B. How can I end my marriage?

A marriage may be ended by dissolution of marriage (the old "divorce"), death of either party, or "nullity of marriage" - the old "annulment."

C. Can I get an annulment?

A nullity judgment is granted automatically if your marriage is void. For example, if you or your spouse were already married to someone else or if you marry a close relative, the court will find that your marriage was "void ab initio," which means that it did not even exist in the beginning.

Another type of nullity is available for what is called a "voidable" marriage. It can be obtained if one of the spouses at the time of the marriage was under age, had a former spouse living but believed him or her to be dead, was of unsound mind, or was physically incapable of living as husband and wife. It is also possible to obtain a nullity if your consent to the marriage was obtained by force. For example, if somebody attacks you on the street, puts a gun to your ribs, and drags you to the altar, you can undo that marriage - unless you voluntarily lived as husband and wife after the force ended.

None of these factors occur frequently. Most people who want a nullity claim some type of fraud. Perhaps your spouse claimed to be rich and you married based upon this representation, which afterward turned out to be false. You may have grounds for a nullity. But expect a battle. Nobody will ever agree to a judgment based on fraud. It is a taint similar to a criminal conviction. And it isn't necessary, because you can get a dissolution of marriage on the grounds of irreconcilable differences simply by testifying to that fact.

D. "Palimony" claims

In the case of *Marvin v. Marvin*,[3] the California Supreme Court held that people who had lived together, whether or not they represented themselves to be married, would have access to the courts to resolve their disputes. It really did not say anything else. This case overruled older law based on the idea that the court would not listen to complaints of unmarried "living togethers." Indeed that law was archaic and sexist. It penalized the woman who had "sinned" while rewarding the man who had also "sinned."[4]

Now the courts can fashion broad remedies: If the parties agreed to share debts and assets, the courts will enforce that agreement. If one party put labor or effort into an asset and was not paid, the court can reconstruct a salary for that party. Or if one party put money into an asset and the title of that asset was held in the other party's name, the courts can remedy that situation also.

But "palimony," or *Marvin* cases as they are known to the legal profession, are few and far between just as are other lawsuits based upon oral contracts. They are hard to prove and expensive. The majority of them occur when the parties have later married and the "Palimony/Marvin" period is filed as a separate suit and tacked onto the dissolution action. Living together is not the way to create marital rights.

E. We would like to have a contract before we get married so that we know where we stand. Are premarital contracts valid?

Clearly, yes. American and international law in business and commerce is based upon the concept of contract. Why shouldn't premarital, antenuptial, or prenuptial (all these words mean the same thing) contracts be valid? The answer is that older premarital contracts were often found to be void on the grounds that they encouraged divorce and that encouraging divorce was against public policy.

But all that changed in 1976 when the California Supreme court held that an antenuptial agreement was no longer automatically suspect.[5] This is what happened:

Betty was an elementary school teacher and **James** was an engineer. They met in 1961 and maintained an "intimate relationship" until March of 1964 when Betty discovered she was pregnant. After many threats on both sides, they married, entering into an agreement disclaiming community property rights. James agreed to support Betty for a minimum period of fourteen calendar months. He also agreed to support their child. The parties remained together eight years.

At their divorce trial, Betty claimed the agreement was void because uncontradicted evidence showed it was not entered into in contemplation of marriage to last until death. The Court found no community property, did not award support, and stated: "An antenuptial agreement violates the policy favoring marriage only insofar as its terms encourage or promote dissolution of marriages." That is, an agreement itself is all right, just don't say that one party will get a million dollars upon dissolution when they have only $100 or so. *That*, according to the courts would encourage divorce.

Premarital agreements are now governed by statute and will generally be upheld, if the parties freely enter into them.[6] There are certain exceptions. Your obligation to support your children is absolute and cannot be contracted away, as is your obligation to support your spouse during the marriage. The statute contains detailed circumstances of when the agreements can be set aside, generally when there is nondisclosure of property or basic unfairness.

Don't try to present your prospective spouse with such a document just before she starts down the aisle - or even after the wedding invitations are out. Aside from being woefully bad judgment and timing, contracts executed when emotions are very high are less likely to be upheld than those executed in a lawyer's office. If you plan a traditional family - that is, husband employed and wife unemployed and caring for children - think about whether a prenuptial agreement in which each party keeps his/her own earnings as separate property could be unfair to the spouse who doesn't have earnings.

Prenuptial agreements have significant advantages. They get you talking about what you want your financial arrangements to be. They let you know the thinking of your "intended" about how you fit into his or her financial scheme. And if you just cannot stand that thinking, it is better to know about it *before* and not *after* the marriage.

II. Community Property

A. What is community property?

The California Family Law Act defines community property[7] as: "All real property situated in this state and all personal property wherever situated acquired during the marriage by a married person while domiciled in this state." The opposite of community property is separate property. That is defined as all property acquired before the marriage, the interest and profits on the separate property, as well as all inheritances, whenever received. We will discuss separate property in Section III.

B. I have many questions about management and responsibility during the marriage.

1. Who manages community property during the marriage?

Since 1975, either spouse can manage community property, except that the person who runs a business has the primary management of that business.[8]

2. What responsibility do we have to each other during the marriage?

The law has changed substantially in this area since the original edition of this book. The responsibility of the manager has ranged from "good faith" to "confidential duty" to "fiduciary duty." Each spouse has a claim against the other for a "breach of fiduciary duty" that lessens the non-managing spouse's interest in his or her community property. The law is not absolutely clear what all those words mean, but don't burn down your house to keep your spouse from getting his/her share. You won't get away with it. The best that will happen is you will burn only your share and have to pay one-half of the total value to your spouse. The worst is that you may additionally suffer substantial fines and other penalties.

C. What constitutes community property?

Community property is all property acquired during the marriage unless it is separate property, inherited, received as a gift or owned before marriage. There are many different types of community property.

1. Miscellaneous personal property

This category includes practically everything that can be considered an asset: furniture, automobiles, jewelry, personal effects, furs, tools, guns, insurance policies, copyrights, patents, licensing agreements, right to receive royalties, club memberships, stocks, bonds, cash, money in the bank, promissory notes or money owed to a spouse, tax refunds, and anything else of value. Only personal property that is community property can be divided. The silver cup you won for placing first in your high school golf tournament is your separate property (unless you were married then).

2. Pensions and retirement funds

"Pensions" (defined as a right to a regular future income from the time of the beginning of a person's retirement to death - and derived from the person's employment) have become one of the biggest property rights in this country. They are important not only in terms of billions of dollars, but also because of the degree of public protection of that right.

Pensions also have become a big issue on the divorce scene. No divorcing spouses, who have been looking forward to a comfortable retirement income, want to give up their share of that income for their later years. The employee-spouse also feels that the retirement income is actually a continuing wage and that any sharing amounts to the same thing as continuing to pay support.

3. Why are pensions included in a discussion of "community property"? Aren't they simply income - and more like wages or salary than like property?

No, they are considered property in the large part because the right to receive the income from the pension fund is a legally enforceable "property right" in the form of a contract which even the government cannot take away. Your feeling that they are income is only a feeling. It is not legally correct.

This concept did not become part of accepted law overnight. California statutes defining property enacted in 1872, (which was borrowed from the New York "Field" code, which was in turn taken from the common law of England) were generally ignored in the pension area in California family law until the case of *In re the Marriage of Brown*[9]

The *Brown* case arose not because pensions were then never divisible, but because one of the techniques for avoiding divisibility in divorces was the uncertainty of payment by the employer, if the pension right was "unvested." In *Brown*, the employee had been with the telephone company some 39 years, and was close to retirement, but the company still called the pension "unvested." At that time it was a common technique for a company to let an employee go just before retirement. The courts in turn treated an unvested pension as an uncertain property right over which they had no jurisdiction in the case of a divorce.

A year or so before *Brown*, in 1974, Congress had enacted a massive statute called ERISA (Employment Retirement Income Security Acts)[10] to protect employees' pension rights against employers and against insolvency of the pension funds. Under ERISA, all pensions had to "vest" (that is, become an absolute right which would survive the discharge of the employee) within ten years, so there was no more firing a loyal employee just before retirement.

The Court in *Brown* said "unvested" pensions were community property and were subject to division on dissolution of the marriage. The leaders in battling for property rights treatment of so-called unvested pensions in divorce cases were lawyers in the forefront of Family Law Specialization.

After *Brown*, employed and retiring spouses sought and found new ways to attack the divisibility of pensions in divorces. And they have done that again and again, even though the law regarding divisibility of community property pensions has been reiterated by the appellate courts hundreds of times. In almost every published pension appeal, it has been the husband attacking the right of the wife to share. That has also been true of a high portion of military men. Several judges' opposition to sharing their own pensions with their own former spouses have also made important law - in favor of the former spouse.

How do I secure a share of my spouse's pension?

If it is a "defined benefit plan," the most common method of dividing pensions is the "time rule." Each party receives a proportionate share of the ultimate income, based on the number of years during the marriage that the pension was earned, and its mathematical relationship to the total number of the years of employment on which the pension income is based. Another method is to have an expert calculate the present value of future income, and then trade the present value of the future income for an asset of equal value, say equity in the family home.

If it is a "defined contribution plan," it is more like a savings account or a profit-sharing plan. The benefit for the employee upon retirement depends upon the value of the employee's account at that time. These plans are generally divided like savings accounts.

What is the thing called a "QDRO?"

QDRO means "Qualified Domestic Relations Order."[11] Congress enacted the governing statute in about 1983 because, among other things, many large corporations, pension plans and unions bitterly fought the division of pensions in divorce, despite state laws requiring division. In almost every divorce in which a pension is divided, your case is not finished until the pension trustee has approved the QDRO.

Some family law lawyers subspecialize in preparing QDROs, and some family law lawyers have the work done by actuaries. Whoever does your QDRO, whether your own family law lawyer or an outside expert, expect the possibility of a large bill. Pension trustees no longer fight the division of the pension, but fight about whether the document your lawyer (or consultant) prepares is or is not a QDRO!

3. Real Property

After personal effects, furniture, and automobiles, the most common type of community real property is the family home. Emotions regarding the family home run high. Although the home itself garners happy (or unhappy) memories and is a haven for the children, the big fight is really over money. If you need two salaries just to scrape the payment together, you will probably want to sell the house at the earliest possible opportunity.

We have a large equity. I want the house sold right away so I can get my money. My spouse wants to stay there with the children because the payments are so low. What will happen in our case?

Under certain circumstances, the court will allow a brief period of residence to the custodial parent, especially if it has been the children's home for some time and the court wants to keep their lives as stable as possible.[12.] If your spouse asks for what is now called a "deferred sale of home order," the Court must first consider whether it is "economically feasible" and if it is, the Court must then look at ten other factors, largely related to the children. So if you and your spouse do not agree on this issue, expect a fight, not only about the delayed sale of the house, but maybe about who should stay in the house and maybe even who should have custody of the children.

The payments on the house are $500 per month. It would rent for $3,000 per month. It is not fair that my spouse can live there after separation without paying me rent.

Under case law known as *In re Marriage of Watts*[13], the community is entitled to rent after separation. Under the facts as you state them, the community would be entitled to $2,500 per month ("rent" of $3,000, less $500 that your spouse is paying to the lender). That means you get $1,250 per month.

For me, it works the other way. I am making payments of $5,000 per month to the lender, and the fair rental value is only $2,000.

Generally, the person in the residence pays the mortgage. Your situation is the exception. You would be entitled to *Epstein*[14] credits in the amount of the difference between the fair rental value and the amount you are paying from your separate property.

I made a large down payment on the house from my savings that had accumulated before our marriage. I want it back, plus interest, plus appreciation. The deed says we both own it. My spouse wants the house to be divided equally. How will the courts view our situation?

For purchases beginning in 1984, a spouse who traces separate property contributions into community property shall be reimbursed for those contributions, unless he/she has given up that right in writing.[15] "Contributions" include down payments, payments for improvements, and payments that reduce the principal of the house mortgage. Payments of interest on the loan or payments made for maintenance, insurance, or house taxes are not included, nor is appreciation or interest on the down payment. So if you bought your house after 1984, you will get your down payment back, but you won't get any interest on the money. All of the increase of value of the property belongs to the community, no matter which one of you made the down payment.

What happens if we bought the house before 1984?

The law before 1984 is a mess. For many years the Legislature and the courts fought a bitter battle. The Legislature would enact a law as described above and the appellate courts would find it unconstitutional as a deprivation of "vested rights."[16] As of this writing, the battle has not been completely resolved. Perhaps a good settlement of this issue would be the procedure described above.

What is the difference between joint tenancy and community property?

Joint tenancy is a concept whereby two persons (who may or may not be related) own property together. The survivor of the two will own the whole property (not just one-half) with no probate intervention on the death of the first. Community property is defined in Section II A above. The deed to your house may describe your ownership as joint tenants. That is probably the result of the title companies using their nationwide preprinted forms. Since community property is a concept which exists in only eight states, it tends to be ignored by the title companies. However, even if your deed says "joint tenancy," Family Code section 2581 makes it community property for all practical purposes in the dissolution of your marriage.

4. Stock Options

If your company has granted you stock options, that is the right to buy company stock at a certain price, and at the date of separation you and your spouse have not exercised them, these options will be divisible to the company during the marriage. They are divided by some complicated formulas, based on whether the options constitute payment for deferred compensation, like pensions, or "golden handcuffs," designed to keep the employee around.

D. What about our business or professional practice? I've heard I might have to share that with my spouse.

Yes, you will, if it is community property. If you are the working or operating spouse, you are going to feel that the business, like a pension, is another stream of income. Again your feeling will not parallel the law. Businesses and professional practices are property, subject to valuation and division on dissolution. Whereas pension law is relatively recent, California courts have been dividing businesses and professional practices for over 100 years.

1. But my business is me. If I leave, the business is gone. How can the courts tell me that I have to share it with my spouse?

Painful as it may be, they are going to do just that. Even though the business may not be worth anything if you leave, it has value to the community as a "going concern." As long as it was "going" at separation, expect it to be valued and divided with your spouse.

2. Tell me then, how it is valued and divided?

A business may be divided "in-kind" (that is, each party would get one-half the business) just as any other asset can be divided. But courts generally prefer to value the business and award one-half of the *value* (as opposed to one-half of the business) to the non-operating spouse, on the theory that divorcing spouses do not make good business partners.

There are several methods to value such a business. Usually, each party employs an expert witness who will testify to its value. The expert is usually an accountant (specializing in Family Law matters, rather than straight accounting) who testifies regularly in court. The expert will take into consideration the following factors:

Gross earnings

A multiple of gross earnings may be used to calculate the value of the business. For example, accounting businesses are often valued at some percentage of the yearly gross.

Good will

This is where the fight is. "Good will" is defined as "an expectation of continued public patronage."[17] Almost every spouse running the business claims it has no good will. Almost every judge finds that it does. So it is best to concentrate on finding out what value will stand up in court, and on appeal if necessary. This is true whether you are the marital partner in charge of the business or the partner who is on the outside.

"Hard Assets"

These include equipment, furniture, cash, accounts receivable minus accounts payable, inventory, leasehold improvements, vehicles, etc. They are appraised in a fashion similar to any other asset.

Other intangibles

Aside from good will, a number of other intangibles exist which include: value of a below-market lease; patents; trademarks and copyrights; customer lists; or anything you can think of that is a part of the money-making capacity of the enterprise. Some Family Law experts even say that the career of a professional athlete is a divisible community asset.

I owned my business before we were married, does that mean it's not community property?

Not necessarily. In Section III we will talk about separate property. The business which you owned before the marriage will be part separate property and part community property. It may require substantial accounting services and litigation to straighten out.

E. Are there other types of community property?

Yes, there are other types of community property which are more or less unusual. Educational and professional licenses are not divisible per se, but under certain circumstances the community can be reimbursed for contributions to education or training of the party that substantially enhanced his/her earning capacity. The procedure to recover education and training expenses is so complex that it is hardly ever used.

Personal injury damages, while community property, are usually assigned to the party who suffered the injuries without any kind of offset.

This is community property that acts more like separate property. The basic concept is that pain and suffering are so personal that they should not be divided with the other spouse.

F. What we have are mostly debts. Are they divided?

Many couples have more debts than assets. Unfortunately, debts are community "property" also, and are to be divided at the same time that the assets are divided. This can work a real inequity on the party who earns little or no money. Making a payment of $1,000 per month will be impossible if you earn only $600.

1. I don't think we can survive. We couldn't pay the bills while we were together, so how do we manage now?

If your finances were strained to the breaking point while you were together and the dissolution of your marriage has caused a total breakdown, sometimes bankruptcy is the only answer. If you decide to do this, you should do it together. Bankruptcy of one spouse only will leave the other spouse with the responsibility for all (not just one-half) of the debts.

2. I'm making payments on all the bills. Can I get credit from my spouse for any of it?

Perhaps. In general, whenever a spouse makes a payment on a community obligation after separation, with separate property funds, that spouse is entitled to reimbursement of one-half of the payment.[18] However, there are some exceptions to this rule. If you intended the payment as a gift, or support, or if the payments were for an asset that you were using (such as your car), there will be no reimbursement. Nor will you get it if the court just thinks it would not be fair.

3. My spouse is threatening to declare bankruptcy. I have good credit. What will happen to me if he/she does?

Most likely you will have to pay all the bills, not just one-half of them. You might want to join in the bankruptcy in order to avoid such a disaster. Alternatively, if there is still jurisdiction to award spousal support, that could be a source of reimbursement for you.

G. How is community property divided?

There are several ways to divide community property. Let's look at each one of them separately:

1. Division in kind

With this method each spouse is awarded a one-half interest in each asset. Some assets, like pensions, are often divided this way. The method is the easiest to calculate, but is generally not favored. Most persons think that spouses, as well as their assets, should be separated after the divorce. For example, imagine the problems of a situation where you own a car together. An example of division in kind is demonstrated in Appendix B.

2. Asset distribution method

The most common method of dividing property is to award (to each party) certain assets and liabilities which are approximately equal to one-half of the total. With the asset distribution method, community assets (minus liabilities) are valued. Each party is then awarded assets which are equal to one-half of the total. This allows a real divorce as each of you will own your own assets free from control of the other. An example is found in Appendix C.

3. Promissory Note

Often you just cannot get the asset distribution method to come out equally. So, in order to accomplish an equal division of community property, the court may require a spouse awarded more than one-half of the community property to execute a secured short-term promissory note in favor of the other spouse. Don't do it unless there is absolutely no alternative, and then demand a reasonable rate of interest, secure it by something (even spousal support), and make it for a short term only. An example of this method is set forth in Appendix D.

4. Sale

Often the court will order the asset or assets sold and the proceeds divided. Judges use this method when there is no other - or when they run out of patience because the parties are fighting. The courts, paid for by the taxpayers, cost us all a lot of money. Most judges feel they should use this limited resource to do something other than listen to spouses fight about the microwave oven or Aunt Minnie's tea set.

My spouse drank/gambled/wasted/stole all of our money. Will the court make him or her repay it to me?

In the first printing of this book the answer was, "Probably not. You may spend more money in attorney's fees than you would ever recover." Now the answer is "probably," and you may be awarded not only attorneys but additional monies if you pursue it. Go back and re-read the section B2. You will need to show your spouse violated his/her fiduciary duty to you in order to win.

H. What is the procedure when our community property is divided?

Property can be divided by a written agreement or an "oral stipulation in open court."[19] The latter means an oral agreement presented by the parties and their attorneys in a formal court setting, which includes the judge, clerk, court reporter and bailiff. The written agreement need not be anything formal. It can even be written on the back of a napkin in a restaurant, as long as it is signed and you intend that it be your agreement for division of property. However, the more formal it is, the easier it will be to enforce and the less likely it will be that things are left out.

J. Are there any taxes on an equal division of community property?

No. There never have been, because an equal division of an asset is a nontaxable event. Before the Internal Revenue Code was amended in 1984,[20] certain equalizing payments were taxable. There are, however, taxes to be paid as a result of events which occur during the dissolution process.

With respect to the family residence, if you have moved out or have been excluded by the court from your residence, you will probably lose your right not to pay taxes on the sale of your principal residence.[21] From this standpoint alone, it might be well to try to stay together until you can buy another house at the same time you sell your former residence.

III. Other Types of Property

A. Separate Property.

The part of the Family Law Act that formally describes separate property is as follows:[22] "All property of the husband or wife, owned by him or her before marriage, and that acquired afterwards by gift, bequest, devise, or descent, with the rents, issues, and profits thereof." This means everything you had before marriage and everything you inherit. You are entitled to keep your separate property during the marriage. And if you do so, upon dissolution, your spouse will not be entitled to any of it.

The courts have also created some special types of separate property. These include disability insurance payments, workers compensation, and other disability pay, as well as personal injury damages for injuries suffered after separation and certain parts of military pensions called "disability" which are in excess of the retirement amounts. Finally, all earnings after your separation are your separate property.[23]

B. I want to keep my separate property separate. What is the biggest problem in trying to do that?

Commingling. Commingling simply means "mixing," mixing your separate property with community property earnings or property, or your spouse's separate property. Commingling can be tantamount to relinquishing your separate property.

1. How does that happen?

Unless you make a specific effort to see that it does not happen, it will. For example, the mere deposit of separate property funds in a joint bank account can constitute commingling. Certainly, multiple deposits, use of separate property funds for community purposes or purchase of assets with commingled funds will almost obliterate the separate status of assets. And, if you run a business or have a professional practice, separate and community interests will automatically be created and commingled just by the marriage.

2. How can I avoid it?

Few married couples avoid commingling of separate property without a clear understanding as to its status. A written agreement is far preferable to anything else. In the absence of a written agreement, keep bank accounts in your own name; never mix with community funds, even if you unmix immediately. If you own real property, use the income from the asset to pay the expenses, and keep the account *separate* from community accounts. If you own stock, keep your trading account *separate* from community trading accounts.

C. So I guess I goofed. I didn't read this book until after I had been married and commingling had occurred. Is there any way I can get any of my separate property returned?

Yes. Indeed, much of the extensive family law litigation is in this area. The general principle is that what is traceable remains separate property. If there is enough money involved, it will be worth trying to trace it. However, be prepared for a fight. You will need extensive accounting services, which may include looking at every check and every transaction which occurred during the marriage.

1. First, tell me how the courts allocate separate and community interests in a family business.

There are two principal approaches. Neither is fool-proof or predictable, but they arise out of two well-known cases:

Pereira Rule

In *Pereira*,[24] the value of the husband's business on the date of the parties' marriage in 1909 was $15,000. At the time of divorce the value was in excess of $70,000. The court allocated a 7% return (the usual interest at that time) on the original investment, and found the balance to be community property. The basic principle in *Pereira* is that labor (time, effort and skill) is community property. The capital, and interest on the capital, of the business remained separate property, even though the husband commingled community property efforts with separate property capital.

Van Camp Rule:

The court in *Van Camp*[25] did just the opposite. Using the same principle that income resulting from services (labor, time, effort and skill) devoted to separate property assets is community property, the court used a different approach: The court first allocated the reasonable value of the services to community property over the period of the marriage, and then treated the balance as normal earnings of the separate property. If you are the spouse who started the marriage owning the business, you will probably want to have the court use the *Van Camp* method, as it results in a larger separate property interest. If you are the other spouse, you will probably seek to have the court apply the *Pereira* approach as it results in a larger community property interest.

2. If it is an asset other than a business, how do I trace separate property?

The best way is by direct tracing. This is accomplished by producing the documents which show the chain or path taken by the separate property funds through various assets. Just go backward from your commingled asset to the separate property asset. This is the exact opposite of the path the funds took into the asset.

For example, if you are trying to trace the down payment into your house, you will need the following documents: Deed to the house, escrow statement showing the down payment, and the canceled check from your separate property bank account in the amount of the down payment. Sometimes funds must be traced through many steps. The number of steps alone does not disqualify the separate property status of the down payment, but the more steps there are, the more confusing it becomes, and the less likely you are to prevail. Your spouse, and the judge, may conclude that you did not successfully trace the funds, or that you transmuted them. (More about transmutation later).

Direct tracing, combined with an indirect method of tracing, called the "family expense method," can solidify separate property status. If payments can be traced to a separate property source by showing that community income at the time of the payments or purchase was used up by family expenses, then the payments or purchase must have been made with separate property funds. That method is expensive, confusing, and not worth doing unless there is a great deal of money at stake.

Under rare circumstances, indirect tracing alone may be sufficient. In 1975 the California Supreme Court reviewed a case[26] involving commingled bank accounts, and said:

   a. Detailed schedules of the spouse showing separate property still remaining in the accounts after purchase of a separate property asset,

   b. *Combined with* her credible testimony that she intended to keep her property separate, was sufficient to trace her separate property.

If you want to keep your separate property separate, you should not rely upon this case. Only direct tracing will assure a good chance of recovery of separate property. And the best way to protect separate property is not to commingle. If you don't commingle, you don't have to trace.

D. What is transmutation?

Transmutation means "the changing or altering in form." Used in the area of community property and separate property, it means to change one into the other. Usually it involves changing separate property to community property - but it could be the reverse. Beginning January 1, 1985, the Family Law Act [27] provides that a transmutation of real or personal property is not valid unless made in writing and including an express declaration of the spouse whose interest in the property is adversely affected. Before that time "pillow talk" - that is, "everything I have is yours" - could be sufficient to cause transmutation. Transmutation takes precedence over tracing. Once it occurs, it changes the character of the asset.

E. My spouse and I have just moved here from another state, where we had substantial property that we acquired during our marriage. We brought it here, but it is all in his/her name. If we had lived here, I think it would have been community property. What can I do about it?

You have what is called "quasi-community property."[28] This means all real or personal property acquired in exactly the way you describe. It was acquired by either spouse living in another state and would have been community property if the spouse who acquired the property had been living in California at the time of its purchase. There are some limitations, however. Both spouses must be domiciled (present and intending to stay) in California at the time of the dissolution action, and the dissolution action must take place in California.

IV. Child Custody

A. What is the basic policy of the law in awarding child custody?

Custody of children is awarded "in the best interests of the children."[29] But what lawyers and mental health professionals think is "in the best interests of the children" differs widely and shifts from one trendy idea to another. Before 1972, it was presumed that children of "tender years" should always go with their mother and children, especially boys, who are of an age to be ready to be trained for a profession or business, should go with their father.

At the present time, the parents come into court on a fairly even footing. If you have been the primary caretaker and wish to continue being so, you have a good chance of that happening. On the other hand, if you have not been the primary caretaker but 1) you are a responsible parent, 2) you establish a living situation appropriate for the children, and 3) you make room in your life for the assumption of much more responsibility than you have previously assumed, you have a chance for sole custody. More probably you will be awarded joint custody, or at least very extended weekend time. Theoretically, courts do not prefer a person because of that person's sex. However, preference is given to the parent who has established a responsible caretaking pattern.

B. What is meant by joint custody?

The statutory definitions have been included in the endnotes,[30] almost verbatim, because no two lawyers or judges will agree on what "joint custody" means. The theory is that children are entitled to continue the same relationship with each parent, notwithstanding the divorce, and almost verbatim, because no two lawyers or judges will agree on what "joint custody" means. The theory is that children are entitled to continue the same relationship with each parent, notwithstanding the divorce, and each parent is entitled to frequent and continuing contacts with the children. Joint custody is very common in California. If parents can live in the same school district and communicate about the rearing of their children in a mature fashion, joint custody is probably good for the children. The old physical custody to the mother and alternate weekends to the father put too much responsibility on the mother and cut off the children too much from the father.

Recent studies are telling parents to carve out a conflict-free zone to work with their children. We all want our children to grow up as emotionally healthy as possible. The less fighting there is over children, the better off they are. Whoever uses the children to fight with the other spouse is going to be in trouble, and may lose custody of them.

C. My husband never paid any attention to the children. He is a drunk/drug addict/ne'er do well/lazy slobbering idiot. I don't ever want him to have anything to do with my children. He only wants to see them so he can pay less money!"

Whoa! If you feel and act this way, you are heading toward the disaster of losing custody of your children. If he was not interested in them while you were married, it is wonderful that he is interested now. Your opportunity to select a different man as your children's father has long since passed, and as much as you think you made a mistake, it is just too late! At the very least, your attitude can cause serious self-esteem and self-confidence problems in your children. No matter what your degree of perfection or his degree of imperfection, he is still their father. If you try to keep the children away from him, they will long for him and idolize him. If he is as bad as you say, set a good example to your children by your behavior, raise them responsibly and give your children credit for coming to an appropriate conclusion about their father themselves. Your attempt to get them to hate him will damage them and back-fire against you. Everybody needs both a father and a mother.

D. Don't be so moralistic! He is all of those things, plus he is now in jail for molesting our children as well as six other children.

Oh! That's different! If you believe your children's safety or health is in jeopardy, you should consult with your attorney.

E. Can there ever be an award to a non-parent?

Hardly ever. If the court finds that an award of custody to a non-parent would be in the best interests of the child and also finds that it would be detrimental to the child to be with either parent, the court can make an award to a non-parent.[31] This can happen when both parents are gravely ill, in jail, refuse to care for the child, or other such extreme situations. It is rare, and the parents always start out with preference.

F. Can a child choose which parent he/she wishes to live with?

Yes. If a child is old enough to make an intelligent decision, based upon mature reasoning, the court will consider it. The court doesn't have to follow the child's wishes. For example, if the child wants to live with Dad because he can watch television there, but Mom makes him do his homework, the court won't pay much attention to the child's wishes.

G. Can I move away with my children?

Maybe. But with the popularity of today's joint custodial arrangements, a parent who wishes to move stands a chance of losing custody of the children. It is the policy of the Legislature to provide "frequent and continuing contacts"[32] between the children and both of their parents. One of the bases in an original award of custody is to award custody of the children to the parent who is more likely to provide those contacts to the other parent. A move is often seen by the court as an attempt to deprive the other parent of those contacts. If you can remain in the same school district as your former spouse - at least while the children are young - you are more likely to be able to continue close contacts with them, whether or not you actually have physical custody.

H. We have a disagreement about who should have custody. We each think the other is a danger to the children. How will the court decide our case?

Before any California judge will hear a word about custody or visitation problems, you must work with a trained mediator (provided by the county and formally known as the "Family Court Services") to try to resolve your custody or visitation differences. Custody mediation will take place no later than your first court appearance. You and your spouse can do it privately if you wish in many California counties. The advantage is that private mediation can continue as long as needed. The Family Court Services has very limited time.

If, after mediation, you cannot reach an agreement regarding your children, the judge or the mediator may recommend an evaluation of the entire family by a mental health professional. If one (or both) of you really is a danger to the children, that will be established in the evaluation and the evaluator will make a recommendation to the judge as to who should have custody.

If, after the evaluation (and perhaps an extended period of mediation), there is still no agreement, a judge may hear your case. However, expect custody litigation to be expensive, prolonged, and painful. Parents who cooperate in the raising of their offspring, whether or not they are married, produce happier, better adjusted children, than do people who fight in court. At least that is current theory, which is backed up by the majority of mental health professionals.

J. We have an irreconcilable difference about custody. Can our children have their own lawyer?

Yes. The court may appoint private counsel[33] to represent the interests of the minor child, if appropriate. This is a new concept and is only as good as the lawyer. If your children get a poor lawyer, the whole case will be much worse than if they did not have one. A good lawyer can often help resolve the dispute before it gets out of control. And your children will feel that somebody is on their side.

K. It looks as if I won't have custody. What kind of visitation will I get?

If physical custody is awarded to your spouse, you will almost always have reasonable rights of visitation. The only exception is if visitation would be detrimental to the child -- that means psychological or physical abuse, not lifestyle disputes. Fights between health food/junk food adherents, religious disputes, disputes about housekeeping, education, when the children should go to bed, what they should wear, or other personal disagreements are not sufficient to cut off visitation. Public policy strongly favors visitation. Sometimes even grandparents can be awarded visitation rights.

L. **We were divorced two years ago and my spouse received physical custody of our children. Now she wants to move away. Can I stop her?**

Probably not. Once physical custody is awarded to one parent, she or he is not required to seek permission of the court to move away with the children. However, there are a number of rules requiring the custodial parent to notify the other parent prior to moving away.

M. **We were divorced two years ago and have shared the children about equally since that time. Our documents provide for joint legal and physical custody. I want to move away with the children. May I?**

No. At least not without a fight. When you have joint physical and legal custody, and one of you wants to move, you go into court with a "de novo" request. That is, your custody dispute is heard just as if you were starting the custody battle from the beginning. Reread the answer to question G above, and be very careful about trying to move away with the children. One distinct possibility is that you will lose custody of your children.

CALIFORNIA DIVORCE

V. Child Support

A. What is basic public policy regarding child support?

Public policy, which is the basis for statutory and case law, provides that both parents have a legal obligation to support their children.[34] Payment of child support is more important than practically anything else, except perhaps taxes. If you are a non-custodial parent, you may have to forget about your credit, payment of bills, even payment of your rent. Your children are more important.

B. How does child support work?

At your first court hearing (see Part I, Section VI), the judge will order the non-custodial parent to pay child (and perhaps spousal) support to the custodial parent. That order will be renewed (or changed) in the judgment of dissolution of marriage. The support will generally be ordered on a monthly basis, usually payable half on the first and half on the fifteenth of the month.

The authority for child support has been part of California Law since California became a state. In the more distant past support awards were low and machinery for their collection was poor. That is still the basic public impression regarding child support, but it is no longer true.

Since at least 1984, because of the strong interrelationship between non-payment of support and welfare, both the federal and state governments now take a strong interest both in providing high awards, and seeing that they are paid. The formula for determining support is found in Family Code section 4055. It is algebraic, complex, and most lawyers do not even bother running the formula by hand. They have some type of computerized system to tell you exactly what support should be set at for your situation.

There are a variety of factors that produce your support level, including the income and taxation status of both parents, the amount of time the children spend with each parent, the number of children in the family, the number of children from other marriages or relationships, extraordinary medical needs of the children, as well as a variety of other factors. Generally, the income of a new spouse or cohabitor is not included in the formula.[35]

C. Does the non-custodial parent have the obligation to pay full support?

No. Both of you have an obligation to support the children. That's occasionally a surprise to some custodial parents. Both fathers *and* *mothers* have an obligation to support the children.

D. I won the lottery and my support, according to the formula, is $25,000 per month. The children cannot possibly use that money, and my "ex" will get a free ride. How can I prevent that?

There is an exception to the high guidelines[36], which gives the court discretion to order less support if "the amount determined under the formula would exceed the needs of the children." However, case law generally provides that the children are entitled to share in the higher standard of living of the non-custodial parent, even though the custodial parent may also benefit. Think about offering to put some of the extra money into a college fund, or some place other than into the hands of the non-custodial parent. But don't be disappointed if the judge awards her/him the full amount of the guideline support as that is within the judge's discretion also.

E. We have joint physical custody. I shouldn't have to pay support, should I?

If your income levels are approximately the same and you spend equal amounts of time with the children, you won't. Otherwise, the California Guidelines assume that the children will spend 20% of their time with the non-custodial parent. If the children spend more time than that with you, or if you have joint custody, that will reduce your obligation, but it probably won't eliminate it.

E. I didn't/couldn't pay for a year. What will happen to me?

If you don't pay any amount ordered, it doesn't go away. It also accumulates interest at the legal rate. It remains a judgment and can be collected any time that you do get some money. If you cannot pay for some reason such as losing your job, you should immediately seek to modify the support. Otherwise you must pay it, if not now, at some time in the future. Modification and Enforcement procedures are described in Part I, Sections X and XI. You should reread those sections to have your questions answered fully.

CALIFORNIA DIVORCE

VI. Spousal Support

A. What is the basic public policy regarding alimony?

The basis for awards of alimony, known as "spousal support" in California (and in this book) is in the Family Law Act, and is reproduced in the endnotes.[37] You should review the endnotes, whether you are the payor spouse or the recipient, because the court, in setting an award of support, is bound to consider the factors required by the Act. But here are some comments:

Public policy does not allow dependent spouses to be thrown onto the street or welfare rolls after a lengthy marriage. But, everybody must work or make a reasonable effort to work. There are no free meal tickets coming out of a marriage. Some older women have been hurt by the Family Law Act, because they left their careers to marry and therefore have minimal skills when they are divorced at age 50 or 60. Spousal support is to help women in this position. If you are substantially younger, expect some kind of salary to be charged to you in the setting of your support, whether or not you actually earn it.

B. That's not what happened to my aunt. Please give me some more background.

There has been an enormous turnaround in attitudes and procedures regarding support in the last three decades. Before 1970, "alimony" was generally awarded to the "innocent wife," if the husband was earning enough to pay it (that meant the woman who was faithful - the" adulterous woman" never received support). In practice, however, alimony was awarded only 20% of the time. Then the court continued to have jurisdiction, i.e., power to modify the support upward or downward.

Immediately after passage of the Family Law Act, between 1970 and 1974, some Courts of Appeal interpreted the Family Law Act as a mandate to relieve long suffering ex-husbands from the continuing burden of support. It tried to "... settle the rights of the parties at one time and ... to some extent curtail endless modification proceedings."[38]

By 1975, however, the courts realized that spousal support is actually necessary to meet the needs of an unemployed homemaker and (although unspoken) to redress the balance in a gender discriminating society. Soon, the appellate courts began saying that support cannot be terminated after a lengthy marriage.

The new Family Law Act has been heralded as:

A bill of rights for harried former husbands who have been suffering under prolonged and unreasonable alimony awards. However, the act may not be used as a handy vehicle for the summary disposal of old and used wives. A woman is not a breeding cow to be nurtured during her years of fecundity, then conveniently and economically converted to cheap steaks when past her prime. If a woman is able to do so, she certainly should support herself. If, however, she has spent her productive years as a housewife and mother and has missed the opportunity to compete in the job market and improve her job skills, quite often she becomes, when divorced, simply a displaced homemaker.[39]

Shortly thereafter, the California Supreme Court, in the case of *In re the Marriage of Morrison*,[40] in somewhat less colorful language, held that in a lengthy marriage the court cannot terminate jurisdiction in the future unless the record clearly indicates that the supported spouse will be able to support herself/himself at the time set for termination. Mrs. Morrison had been married for 27 years and was 54 years old at trial. She had spent her married life as a homemaker and had just begun minimal employment at approximately minimum wage. She did not even drive a car. The trial court awarded support for eleven years, then terminated it. The Supreme Court said that the trial court was not justified in "burning its bridges" into the future.

C. You've used some words I don't understand. Can you define the terms used for spousal support?

Yes, spousal support does involve its own peculiar vocabulary. For example, spousal support can be awarded as "temporary," or "permanent," "until further order of court," a "step-down," a "retention of jurisdiction," a "non-modifiable" award, or no award at all, a "termination." Let's look at these terms:

What is a "lengthy marriage?"

The Family Code[41] provides a presumption that 10 years is a "lengthy marriage."

What is temporary support?

This support, if ordered, may be at the first court hearing (see Part I, Section VI). The purpose of temporary support is to preserve the status quo, pending the resolution of the balance of the issues by trial or settlement[42] For that reason the California Guidelines that we discussed under child support are applicable to spousal support. If there are no children, the award will be approximately 40% of the payor's net income minus 50% of the recipient's net income. This percentage is adjusted if there is child support ordered.

What is "permanent" support?

The purpose of "permanent" spousal support is not to preserve the pre-separation status quo, but to provide financial assistance, if appropriate, as determined by the financial circumstances of the parties after their dissolution and the division of their community property.[43] The computerized guidelines are not supposed to be used. Support is really not "permanent," because unless support is made non-modifiable, it will always be modifiable "upon a proper showing of changed circumstances."

What is a step-down?

A common method of reducing support during the 1970's was to provide support for a period of time, then "step-down" the amount. For example: $1,000 per month for two years, then $500 per month for another two years, then a retention of jurisdiction for two years, then a termination of jurisdiction. This method is uncommon today, and at higher levels of support could trigger very adverse tax consequences to the payor.

Can we make support so it can never be changed?

Yes, that is called "non-modifiable."[44] You and your spouse must agree to it. For example, you can agree that the supported spouse will receive $1,000 per month over a period of five years without any modification under any circumstances. This method is not common, but it can be a good planning device. Both of you have absolute certainty as to the amount and the duration. If you are the payor, before you agree to non-modifiable support, make sure you have adequate resources to pay it - even if you lose your job.

Does jurisdiction go on forever?

"Jurisdiction" means power. A "retention of jurisdiction" means that the court has power to make an award of support. So, even though you are not paying/receiving any money, if the court has retained jurisdiction to make an award of support, you could pay/receive money in the future. The only way to make sure this does not happen is for there to be a termination of jurisdiction.

What does that mean, "termination of jurisdiction?"

This means that the court does not have power to make an award. "Future termination of jurisdiction" means that the court loses power to make an award in the future at the specific date set. The latter, however, is tricky. In some recent cases, some husbands who thought their support would be terminating, found that it didn't happen. If you don't mention termination in your agreement, it will automatically terminate on the supported spouse's remarriage, or the death of either party.

I understand that spousal support can only continue for one-half the length of the marriage. How does that fit in with what we have been talking about?

The public has long perceived that spousal support payments continued for no more than one-half the length of the marriage. In 1996[45] the Legislature incorporated that perception into the Family Code. The statute appears to be somewhat in conflict with *Morrison*, so watch for the appellate courts to straighten it out as soon as the appropriate case presents itself.

D. My spouse received a very substantial property settlement. Will I still have to pay support?

Probably not. In California, property division and spousal support are different issues. But there is an interrelationship based upon need, i.e., if the supported spouse receives one million dollars in property, it is unlikely that she/he will need support. In Southern California the interpretation of "need" may be somewhat different.

E. I'm the payor. And I think that paying support is going to ruin my life. What can I do about it?

You are not alone. The thing that bothers most former spouses about paying support is the interminability of it. But there are a number of remedies.

1. The recipient former spouse can be examined by a vocational evaluator to see what type of work, if any, he or she can do.[46] This procedure can be repeated in future years. That is, there can be a review at specified intervals to see what efforts he/she has made to find employment. If the supported spouse is employed, or employable, that will tend to reduce the support.

2. Sometimes, if there is enough money, it is possible to "buy out" a spousal support award. That is, you can provide a type of annuity for your former spouse with property as well as through monthly payments.

3. All income of your former spouse is taken into consideration in setting the award, not just earnings. If your former spouse has any income-producing property, that will lower the spousal support.

4. If there is just no alternative to it, spousal support is the greatest tax shelter going. Spousal support, known as "alimony" in the tax code[47] is fully deductible to the payor as long as it is paid, with a few exceptions.

F. Describe the tax consequence of paying or receiving spousal support in more detail.

Spousal support is generally deductible to the payor and includible in the income of the recipient. This means that the payor will be in a substantially lower tax bracket than he/she would have been without payment of the support. The recipient will have to report that support as income and pay taxes on it. While there are some limitations on the deductibility of support, they do not occur until you pay more than $15,000 per year. Paying spousal support is usually offensive, but deductibility eases the pain.

CALIFORNIA DIVORCE

Conclusion

I don't like what you described in this book. I don't like the system. What can I do about it?

You are not alone - after all, divorce is an unpleasant process. Many people such as Arnold, Barbara and Chuck, the examples in the introduction, spent a great deal of money fighting with each other and even with their own lawyers. Their dispute, however, may be with the Legislature. The Legislature sets and articulates public policy. If you don't like the public policy, as it is written by the Legislature in The Family Law Act, you can do something to change it.

My goodness, I can't "fight City Hall" and now you are telling me to fight the Legislature?

No, the suggestion is that you work towards the formation of new laws more to your liking. Review the very first chapter where we talked about "What is law." Don't try to make your changes through the court system, as that route is lengthy, expensive, time-consuming, and uncertain. But you have an opportunity through the Legislature. Three examples follow:

1. During the early 1970's, several women's groups were enraged by the imposition of equal responsibility on divorcing women. Women were obligated to get out and work long before there were equal opportunities to do so. These groups set out to change California's

sexist laws. One statute said something like: "The husband is the head of the family; he may choose any reasonable place and mode of living and the wife must conform thereto." Another gave the husband management and control of community property - no matter if he was not good with money and she was a successful financial planner. These women forced the Legislature to repeal the first law and to change management and control so that either spouse now has management and control rights of the community property.

2. In the early 1980s, a group of men, lonely and unhappy without their children after their divorces, banded together to form the organization "Equal Rights For Fathers." This organization succeeded in convincing the Legislature to adopt the current joint custody statutes and to set the policy of "frequent and continuing contacts" as part of California's public policy.

3. Every year many Family Law lawyers, leaders in their profession, spend countless hours before the Legislature testifying, lobbying, and working towards the improvement of the Family Law Act. In 1984, when Congress imposed dreadful limitations on tax deduction for "alimony" (spousal support), it was Family Law Specialists who convinced the California Legislature not to conform. ("Conform" with respect to federal and state taxation statutes means that California adopts a similar statute to that passed by Congress.) Their work may have indirectly convinced Congress to repeal the bulk of those unfair limitations in 1986.

So, you can make a difference. In the first edition of this book, I asked some questions that now have answers:

1. "Would you like to see more teeth in Family Law enforcement, such as automatic wage assignments for child support?" Automatic wage assignments for both child and spousal support are now the law.

2. "Do you think (or not think) that a delayed sale of the family residence is always appropriate?" Both the courts and the Legislature have struggled with this concept over the last ten years.

3. "Would you like to see Family Law handled only by specialized

judges in Family Courts?" While not all courts in California have separate family law departments, probably more than one-half do now. That was an almost unknown concept nine years ago.

If you want something else, contact your State Senator or Assembly Representative. You probably know them from the times that they rang your doorbell and asked for your vote. Now it is your turn to ask for a favor. If you are part of a group, that is even better. Work with your Representative through your local organization.

I still feel as if it's a no-win deal. I still don't like it.

Nobody does. The legal aspects of a divorce tend to intensify the feelings of personal loss which you are suffering. Before the Family Law Act, the emphasis was not on finances, as it is now, but on the cause or "fault" of the breakup. Although you could tell about how you had been hurt then, you also had to deal with your spouse telling his or her story about how he or she had been hurt. That was called "slinging mud." It could and did destroy people's lives.

The Family Law Act was intended to restore dignity to the court room and allow marriages to end without people tearing each other limb from limb as they were able to do before. It stopped the use of our precious court resources for airing what should be private fights. Whatever other problems The Family Law Act has generated, anyone who can remember the circuses that occurred before 1970 agrees that the "no fault" concept of the Act has been a great success in achieving its intended goals. So divorce should be less painful now, at least emotionally, than it was before the Family Law Act.

Divorce is still miserable because it is impossible to divide any sum of money by two and make anyone happy. You (and everyone else) are accustomed to the benefits of both salaries (or all the salary if there is only one), and the benefits of all the assets. Dividing salaries and assets causes a reduction in everybody's standard of living. The old saying that "two can live as cheaply as one," may be true. Certainly when the "two" become two, rather than "one," there are many more expenses. But the legal process cannot help you with this problem. It does not create new wealth; it only decides how to slice the existing pie.

Do you have any other suggestions as to how I can escape this process?

Certainly. Communicate with each other before the marriage. What lifestyle do each of you want? What do you expect of each other? If you cannot agree prior to the marriage, your chances of success after the marriage are not good. Ask each other, "What type of settlement would you want if we divorced?" If your spouse-to-be says, "You could have the clothes on your back, and I would get everything else," then you might want to consider marrying someone else.

If your "intended" has been through a nasty divorce, and has told you many tales about it, you might want to go to the county where the divorce occurred and read the file - which is a matter of public record. There could be many benefits to this action for you, not the least is that you could determine whether he/she is telling you the truth. If you are in the midst of a conflicted divorce, remember, anybody, including a potential new partner or an employer can learn a lot about you from your file. Try not to do anything, or take any position which you would be ashamed of later.

Is there a positive side to the divorce process?

Yes, there is. The purpose of Family Law proceedings is (and always has been) to provide justice and equity to husband and wife, to the minor children, and to society. The family, which is still the basic unit of our society, is not dissolved by the dissolution of the marriage -- only changed in form. Public policy continues to protect that basic unit. The Family Law Act structures that protection to be most fair to all the parties and to be of maximum benefit to the people of California.

Another positive aspect about the dissolution process is that it doesn't last forever. The legal process is truly a maze -- you must enter and go through it to get out. Once out, you can reconstruct your life and move forward. You couldn't do that when you were in an unsatisfactory marriage.

If this book has helped you understand how to work with the legal system - if it makes your life in any way easier, more pleasant, or less expensive - we have fulfilled our purpose.

Endnotes

Part I

1. California Family Code.
2. Statutory authority for restraining orders is found in Family Code sections 6200 et seq. (Domestic Violence Prevention Act), Family Code section 6320 et seq., Family Code section 241, and Family Code section 2047.
3. Family Code section 2040(a)
4. In Re Marriage of Baragry (1977) 73 Cal.App.3d 444, 140 Cal.Rptr. 779.
5. Code of Civil Procedure section 657
6. Code of Civil Procedure section 663
7. Code of Civil Procedure section 1008
8. Code of Civil Procedure section 473

Part II

1. California Family Code.
2. Family Code Section 2310.
3. Marvin v. Marvin, (976) 18 Cal.3d 660, 134 Cal.Rptr.815
4. Keene v. Keene (1962) 57 Cal.2d 657, Cal.Rptr. 593.
5. In Re Marriage of Dawley (1976) 17 Cal.3d 342, 131 Cal.Rptr. 3.
6. Family Code Section 1612 et.seq.
7. Family Code Sections 760, 1100.
8. Family Code section 1100 (d).
9. In Re Marriage of Brown (1976) 15 Cal.3d 838, 126 Cal.Rptr. 633.
10. Internal Revenue Code Section 401 et.seq. 29 U.S.C. 1001 et.seq.
11. Internal Revenue Code section 414(p)
12. Family Code section 3800
13. In Re Marriage of Watts (1985) 171 cal.App.3d 366, 217 CalRptr. 301
14. In Re Marriage of Epstein (1979) 24 Cal.3d 76, 154 Cal.Rptr. 413.
15. Family Code Sections 2581, 2640.
16. In Re Marriage of Buol (1984) 39 Cal.3d 751, 218 Cal.Rptr. 31.
17. Business and Professions Code Section 14100.
18. In Re Marriage of Epstein (1979) 24 Cal.3d 76, 154 Cal.Rptr. 413.
19. Family Code Section 2550.
20. Internal Revenue Code section 1041.
21. Internal Revenue Code Section 1034(a).
22. Family Code Section 770.
23. Family Code Section 771.
24. Pereira v. Pereira (1909) 156 Cal. 1, 103 P. 488.
25. Van Camp v. Van Camp (1921) 53 Cal.App. 17, 371 P.2d 745.

26. In Re Marriage of Mix (1975) 14 Cal.3d 604, 122 Cal.Rprt. 79.
27. Family Code Section 852.
28. Family Code Section 2641; In Re Marriage of Roesch (1978) 83 Cal.App.3d 96, 147 Cal.Rprt.586.
29. Family Code Section 3020.
30. Family Code Sections 3002, 3007, 3004, 3006, 3003 are reproduced as follows:
    1. "Joint Custody" means joint physical custody and joint legal custody. (3002)
    2. "Sole physical custody" means that a child shall reside with and be under the supervision of one parent, subject to the power of the court to order visitation. (3007)
    3. "Joint physical custody" means that each of the parents shall have significant periods of physical custody. Joint physical custody shall be shared by the parents in such a way so as to assure a child of frequent and continuing contact with both parents. (3004)
    4. "Sole legal custody" means that one parent shall have the right and the responsibility to make the decisions relating to health, education, and welfare of a child. (3006)
    5. "Joint legal custody" means that both parents shall share the right and the responsibility to make the decisions relating to health, education, and welfare of a child. (3003)
31. Family Code Section 3041 provides as follows: Before making an order granting custody to a person or persons other than a parent,, without the consent of the parents, the court shall make a finding that granting custody to a parent would be detrimental to the child and that granting custody to a nonparent is required to serve the best interests of the child.
32. Family Code Section 3020 provides as follows: The Legislature finds and declares that it is the public policy of this state to assure minor children frequent and continuing contacts with both parents after the parents have separated or dissolved their marriage, and to encourage parents to share the rights and responsibilities of child rearing in order to effect this policy, except where the contact would not be in the best interest of the child, as provided in Section 3011.
33. Family Code Section 3150.
34. Family Code Section 4001 et.seq.
35. Family Code section 4057.5
36. Family Code section 4057(b)(3)
37. Family Code Section 4320

Circumstances to be considered in ordering spousal support. In ordering spousal support under this part, the court shall consider all of the following circumstances:

(a) The extent to which the earning capacity of each party is sufficient to maintain the stand of living established during the marriage, taking into account all of the following:

(1) The marketable skills of the supported party; the job market for those skills; the

time and expense required for the supported party to acquire the appropriate education or training to develop those skills; and the possible need for retraining or education to acquire other, more marketable skills or employment.

(2) the extent to which the supported party's present or future earning capacity is impaired by periods of unemployment that were incurred during the marriage to permit the supported party to devote time to domestic duties.

(b) the extent to which the supported party contributed to that attainment of an education, training, career position, or a license by the supporting party. (c) the ability to pay of the supporting party, taking into account the supporting party 's earning capacity, earned and unearned income, assets, and standard of living. (d) the needs of each party based on the standard of living established during the marriage. (e) the obligations and assets, including the separate property, or each party. (f) the duration of the marriage. (g) the ability of the supported party to engage in gainful employment without unduly interfering with the interest of dependent children in the custody of the party. (h) The age and health of the parties. (i) The immediate and specific tax consequences to each party. (j) b *The balance of the hardships to each party. (k) The goal that the supported party shall be self-supporting within a reasonable period of time. A "reasonable period of time" for purposes of this section generally shall be one-half the length of the marriage. However, nothing in this section is intended to limit the court's discretion to order support for a greater or lesser length of time, based on any of the other factors listed in the section and the circumstances of the parties.* (l) any other factors the court determines are just and equitable.

38. In Re Marriage of Patrino, 36 Cal.App.3d 186, 111 Cal.Rptr 367.
39. In Re Marriage of Brantner (1977) 67 Cal.App.3d 416, 136 Cal.Rptr 635.
40. In Re Marriage of Morrison (1978) 20 Cal.3d 437,143 Cal.Rptr. 139.
41. Section 4336 (b)
42. In Re Marriage of Burlini (1983) 143 Cal.App.3d 65, 191 Cal.Rptr. 541.
43. Burlini, supra (see note 37).
44. Family Code Section 3591(c).
45. Family Code section 4330, now provides as follows: "When making an order for spousal support,... the court shall give the parties the following admonition: "It is the goal of this state that each party shall make reasonable good faith efforts to become self-supporting as provided for in Section 4320. The failure to make reasonable good faith effort, may be one of the facts considered by the court as a basis for modifying or terminating support."
46. Family Code Section 4331.
47. Internal Revenue Code Sections 71 and 215.

Appendix A

Personal Information of Wife

1. Name: _____

2. Present address: _____

3. Social Security number: _____

4. Length of stay in California:_____

5. Birthplace: _____

6. Occupation: _____

7. Present employment: _____

8. Current gross monthly salary: _____

If wife has income other than from salary, please set it forth in detail on additional sheets.

9. Highest school grade completed: _____

10. Date and place of marriage: _____

11. County of marriage: _____

12. Residence at time of separation: _____

13. Date of separation: _____

14. Names, birthplaces & birth dates of living children of this marriage:

_____   _____

_____   _____

_____   _____

15. Number of previous marriages terminated by:

Death: _____   Legal proceedings: _____

16. Name (s) of former spouse(s):

_____   _____

Personal Information of Husband

1. Name: _____

2. Present address: _____

3. Social Security number: _____

4. Length of stay in California: _____

5. Birthplace: _____

6. Occupation: _____

7. Present employment: _____

8. Current gross monthly salary: _____

If husband has income other than from salary, please set it forth in detail on additional sheets.

9. Highest school grade completed: _____

10. Date and place of marriage: _____

11. County of marriage: _____

12. Residence at time of separation: _____

13. Date of separation: _____

14. Names, birthplaces & birth dates of living children of this marriage:

_____   _____

_____   _____

_____   _____

15. Number of previous marriages terminated by:

   Death: _____   Legal proceedings: _____

16. Name (s) of former spouse(s):

_____   _____

MONTHLY EXPENSES

	Yourself alone	Yourself & children
1. Residence		
a. Rent or mortgage	$_____	$_____
b. Real property taxes	$_____	$_____
c. Homeowner's or renter's insurance	$_____	$_____
d. Maintenance & fees	$_____	$_____
3. Food at home & household supplies	$_____	$_____
4. Food eaten out	$_____	$_____
5. Utilities	$_____	$_____
6. Telephone	$_____	$_____
7. Laundry & cleaning	$_____	$_____
8. Clothing	$_____	$_____
9. Medical & dental	$_____	$_____
10. Insurance (life, accident, etc. Do not include auto, home, health insurance	$_____	$_____
11. Child care	$_____	$_____
12. Education (specify)	$_____	$_____
13. Entertainment	$_____	$_____
14. Transportation & auto expenses	$_____	$_____
15. Installment payments	$_____	$_____
16. Incidentals	$_____	$_____
17. TOTAL MONTHLY EXPENSES	$_____	$_____

PROPERTY DATA

The items that are starred (**) require documents:

I. Real estate - Attach the following for each property:
   ** 1. Copy of the closing escrow statement
   ** 2. Copy of the original deed to you
   ** 3. Copy of latest lender's statement

Please answer the following questions about real estate. Attach additional sheets if necessary:

	Property #1	Property #2
Address:	_____	_____
	_____	_____
How title held (exact):	_____	_____
Purchase date:	_____	_____
Down payment:	$_____	$_____
Source of down payment (your or your spouse's or other funds):	_____	_____
Estimated present market values:	$_____	$_____
Loan balance:		
1st trust deed:	$_____	$_____
2nd trust deed:	$_____	$_____
Monthly payments:		
1st trust deed:	$_____	$_____
2nd trust deed:	$_____	$_____
To whom payable:		
1st trust deed:	_____	_____
2nd trust deed:	_____	_____

If you do not have these documents, a copy of any recorded document (such as a deed) can be obtained at the County Recorder's office. Your lawyer can get them for you. But it will be less expensive if you do so yourself.

II. Furniture

** Attach a list of furniture, specifying those items you believe to be separate property, and your opinion of the value of each item.

III. Jewelry, furs, and other valuable items

** Attach a list of valuable items and specify those items you believe to be separate property, and your opinion of the value of each.

IV Vehicles

** A. Automobiles, motorcycles, boats, etc. Attach a copy of registration for each (title document).

	# 1	# 2	# 3
Year:	_____	_____	_____
Make:	_____	_____	_____
Model:	_____	_____	_____
How title held:	_____	_____	_____
Loan balance:	_____	_____	_____
Monthly payments:	_____	_____	_____
To whom payable:	_____	_____	_____
Date Acquired:	_____	_____	_____
Source of down payment:	_____	_____	_____

V. Cash assets

Deposits (indicate amount, location, account number, in whose name held and where the money came from.) **For each account for which you have a passbook, statement or other document, attach a copy of the latest statement and statement as of date-of-separation.

A. Savings accounts

_____

_____

B. Checking accounts

_____

_____

C. Credit Union or other

_____

_____

D. Cash – give location.

_____

_____

VI. Life insurance policies

**Attach a copy of the declaration page for each policy. For each policy set forth: (Use additional sheets if necessary.)

A. Name of Insurer:_____

B. Policy Number: _____

C. Type of Insurance:_____

D. Explain the benefits (or attach copy of that policy)

_____

_____

VII. Stocks and mutual funds

For all stock held indicate name of company, number of shares, whether common, preferred or other, cost of acquisition, date acquired, present value, how title is held, source of purchase price.
**ATTACH A COPY OF THE STOCK CERTIFICATE OR THE LATEST STATEMENT FROM YOUR BROKER. Use extra sheets if necessary.

Name of Company _____

Title Holder _____

Number of Shares _____ Common _____ Preferred _____

Cost of Acquisition _____ Date Acquired _____

Present Value _____Source of Purchase Price_____

VIII. Bonds

For all bonds held indicate date of acquisition, issuer, type, date of maturity, face amount, how title is held, source of purchase price.
**PLEASE ATTACH A COPY OF THE BOND OR THE LATEST STATEMENT FROM YOUR BROKER. (Use extra sheets if necessary.)

Issuer _____

Type _____ Date of Maturity _____

Face Amount _____ Date of Acquisition _____

Title _____

Source of Purchase Price _____

IX. Retirement, pension, profit-sharing, annuities, IRA's, Deferred compensation.
**ATTACH COPY OF LATEST PLAN SUMMARIES AND LATEST BENEFIT STATEMENT.

** A. Pension rights of you and/or spouse

** B. Profit sharing plans

** C. IRA's (Individual Retirement Accounts)

** D. Annuities

X. Receivables
Does anybody owe you any money? If so, indicate amount, date acquired, name of debtor and payment provisions.
**ATTACH A COPY OF THE PROMISSORY NOTE.

XI. Business interests of you or your spouse
**ATTACH COPY OF MOST CURRENT K-1 FORM AND SCHEDULE C.

	Interest #1	Interest #2
Name of interest:	_____	_____
Type of Business:	_____	_____
Corporation, partner-ship, sole ownership:	_____	_____
Percentage owned:	_____	_____
Name in which title is held:	_____	_____
Annual net income:	_____	_____
**Buyout agreements: (Attach copy)	_____	_____

XII. Miscellaneous

Do you or your spouse have any of the following?

1. Stock options   yes_____   no_____

2. Oil royalties   yes_____   no_____

3. Investment interests   yes_____   no_____

4. Club memberships   yes_____   no_____

5. Option rights   yes_____   no_____

6. Trusts (settlor, trustee, beneficiary,
   principal and income; if you or spouse
   are the settlor, state date of trust set up,
   source of funds, date of termination)   yes_____   no_____

7. Legacies or bequests
   receivable from probate estates   yes_____   no_____

8. Personal injury causes of action   yes_____   no_____

9. Copyright ownership (literary
   musical, etc.)   yes_____   no_____

10. Patent ownerships   yes_____   no_____

11. Licensing agreements as licensor   yes_____   no_____

12. Licensing agreements as licensee   yes_____   no_____

13. Rights to receive royalties   yes_____   no_____

14. Other contractual rights   yes_____   no_____

If the answer to any of the above is "yes" please describe on additional sheets.
    ** Documents required

XIII. Separate Property

A. Did you have any money or property at the time of your marriage? If so, where is it now? Set forth detailed list if still in existence.

B. Did your spouse have any money or property at the time of marriage? If so, where is it now? Set forth a detailed list.

Taxes

** Attach copies of the last five years tax returns.

Do you expect a tax refund this year?

     Yes_____   No_____

If so, how much? _____

Are any back taxes due to either the state or federal government?

     Yes_____   No_____

If so, how much? _____

Debts and Liabilities

** ATTACH A COPY OF THE STATEMENT OR BILL OF EVERY CREDITOR AT THE DATE CLOSEST TO SEPARATION. THIS IS EXTREMELY IMPORTANT!

Creditor	Purpose Incurred	Amt. Due at separation	Balance due now	Monthly payment
_____	_____	_____	_____	_____
_____	_____	_____	_____	_____
_____	_____	_____	_____	_____
_____	_____	_____	_____	_____
_____	_____	_____	_____	_____
_____	_____	_____	_____	_____
TOTALS		_____	_____	_____

Appendix B
Equal Division of Each Asset

Description	Gross	Encumbrance	Net	Wanda	Hank
Family residence	200,000	105,800	94,200	47,100	47,100
Mercedes	12,000	5,400	6,600	3,300	3,300
Honda SXK	4,000	1,600	2,400	1,200	1,200
Stock	10,000	0000	10,000	5,000	5,000
Apt. building	500,000	150,000	350,000	175,000	175,000
Wanda's pension	68,000	0000	68,000	34,000	34,000
Furniture	5,000	0000	5,000	2,500	2,500
National Savings	26,000	0000	26,000	13,000	13,000
Hank's business	125,000	0000	125,000	62,500	62,500
TOTALS	950,000	262,800	687,200		
ONE HALF			343,600	343,600	343,600

Appendix C
Asset Distribution Method

Description	Gross	Encumbrance	Net	Wanda	Hank
Family residence	200,000	105,800	94,200	94,200	0000
Mercedes	12,000	5,400	6,600	0000	6,600
Honda SXK	4,000	1,600	2,400	2,400	0000
Stock	10,000	0000	10,000	0000	10,000
Apartment building	500,000	150,000	350,000	175,000	175,000
Wanda's pension	68,000	0000	68,000	68,000	0000
Furniture	5,000	0000	5,000	4,000	1,000
National Savings	26,000	0000	26,000	0000	26,000
Hank's business	125,000	0000	125,000	0000	125,000
TOTALS	950,000	262,800	687,200	343,600	343,600
ONE HALF			343,600	343,600	343,600

Appendix D
Combination:
Including Promissory Note
and Unsecured Debts

Description	Gross	Encumbrance	Net	Wanda	Hank
Family residence	200,000	105,800	94,200	94,200	0000
Mercedes	12,000	5,400	6,600	0000	6,600
Honda SXK	4,000	1,600	2,400	2,400	0000
Stock	10,000	0000	10,000	10,000	0000
Apartment building	500,000	150,000	350,000		350,000
Wanda's pension	68,000		68,000	68,000	0000
Furniture	5,000		5,000	4,000	1,000
Hank's business	125,000		125,000	0000	125,000
Community Obligations		[40,000]	[40,000]		[40,000]
SUB-TOTALS	924,000	302,800	621,200	178,600	442,600
EQUALIZING PAYMENT			310,600	132,000	[132,000]
TOTALS				310,000	310,000

115

NOTES